ISBN 978-0-428-73427-5
PIBN 10175731

"Great Writers."

EDITED BY

PROFESSOR ERIC S. ROBERTSON, M.A.

LIFE OF ADAM SMITH.

OF

ADAM SMITH

BY

R. B. HALDANE, M.P.

———— ————

LONDON

WALTER SCOTT

24 WARWICK LANE, PATERNOSTER ROW

1887

(All rights reserved.)

CONTENTS.

———•◦•———

CHAPTER I.

CHAPTER II.

CHAPTER III.

CHAPTER IV.

CHAPTER V.

LIFE OF ADAM SMITH.

———◆———

CHAPTER I.

IT is more difficult to write about a man of letters than about any other kind of great man. The individuality of an author, to whatever extent he may live in the creations of his pen, is immensely less bound up, in the public imagination, with his deeds, than is that of a soldier or a statesman. If these deeds have fashioned our daily lives, they have done so in a manner usually far more subtle and less obvious in the former case than in the latter.

The individuality of Adam Smith can hardly be said to be bound up at all with his deeds. Even in Kirkcaldy and Edinburgh, the places of his birth and of his death, but little memorial of him has survived. We think of him, in the main, and we think of him rightly, as the bosom friend of David Hume. It is to be regretted, on nearly all scores, that the records of his life are so meagre. For he was a great writer, and an interesting man. He is not reputed to have played any part in the world's history of the kind which tempts those whose ambition it is to show that the private and inner lives of all men are lived on a level. On the contrary, he was a somewhat shy, retiring, and awkward student, caring, so far as we can judge, little what the world thought about himself, and much what it thought, or some day would think, of his books. To give some account of the life and work of this man, without magnifying or diminishing either unduly, is the object aimed at in these pages. In order to do so at all fairly, within the compass of a small space, it will be necessary, so far as possible, to abstract from irrelevant detail, and to invite the attention of the reader to more marked and distinctive matters.

To the practical politician and social reformer, Adam Smith ought to be a hero, no less than he is to the economist. To both he appears in the light of one of the greatest vanquishers of error on record, the literary Napoleon of his generation. No man in modern times has said more with so much effect within the compass of one book. Yet it is not probable that any competent person could now be found to repeat without hesitation the assertion, made more than once by Buckle in his "History of Civilization," that "The Wealth of Nations" is the most important book ever written. As we become removed by an ever-increasing distance from the prejudices and opinions which Adam Smith once for all shattered, their magnitude and importance appear to grow smaller. It is safe to affirm that even the battle between Free Trade and Protection will never again be fought upon the ground from which Smith drove his opponents. Here, as in almost every other particular, the controversies of political economy turn upon new issues, however they may resemble the old disputes in name.

Adam Smith was a breaker down of prejudices. What the prejudices were which the Time-spirit equipped him to encounter, it will be the chief business of this volume to state in a plain fashion. Like every great thinker he came upon a scene which was prepared for him. Like every great thinker he is apt to lose something of the admiration he merits, because of the extent to which his conceptions have entered into and become part of our intellectual lives.

The economist possesses a certain advantage over the metaphysician and the man of letters. His department of knowledge is not old enough to have had periods of want of progress, and even of backward movement. He has not to torment himself by observing how much less the Greeks were embarrassed by conceptions, such as that of the distinction of subject and object, which to-day hinder us by thrusting themselves with irresistible force upon philosopher and man of letters alike. His is an unbroken history of advances in the direction of intellectual freedom. It is with the name of Adam Smith that the most important of these advances are associated. His work was something more than the overthrow of the agricultural and mercantile systems, and the extirpation of certain subtle prejudices derived from the doctrines of these systems by persons who did not in terms profess them. He threw the lessons of modern political economy into a systematic form, and thereby left them advanced a stage in their development.

It is as an economist that Smith will be remembered.

For the right understanding of his great book, and of how it came to be that his teaching was something more than a mere theory of the production and distribution of wealth, it must never be forgotten that he was also a writer on Ethics, and would, had he carried out his intentions, have been a writer on Jurisprudence as well.

But while the subject matter of "The Wealth of Nations" formed part of the systematic course, embracing all these three subjects, which its author was accustomed to deliver to his students in the University of Glasgow, on it alone depends the great position of him who wrote it. His contribution to Ethics was, as we shall see, unimportant, and of that made by him to Jurisprudence we have no sufficient record to enable us to form a judgment.

How, and out of what materials, "The Wealth of Nations" was fashioned, will best be understood after we have seen what kind of man its author was.

CHAPTER II.

KIRKCALDY, or as the name was spelt in the days of Adam Smith, Kirkaldy, is a manufacturing town on the north side of the Firth of Forth. From its peculiar characteristic of possessing great length without breadth, it has for generations enjoyed the appellation of "the lang toon." The inhabitants are of that shrewd, hard-headed nature for which Fife is famous. Manufacture overshadows agriculture, and the general aspect of the place is that of industry. Judging of the past, not merely from tradition, but by the present, Kirkcaldy is an ideal place of nurture for economists.

It was in this town that Smith was born on June 5, 1723, three months after the death of his father. That father had originally been a member of the Society of Writers to the Signet, a branch of the legal profession which has no counterpart out of Scotland. Performing most of the functions of solicitors (in this country a distinct body), and at the same time of conveyancing counsel, a very large portion of the occupation of the Writers to the Signet consisted, then as now, in the management of the estates of the more important of the Scottish landed gentry, an occupation which sometimes brought them into close, and often confidential, relationships with distinguished public men. It was, therefore, not unnatural that Smith's father should quit his profession for the private secretaryship to the Earl of Loudoun, the Principal Secretary of State for Scotland, and Keeper of the Great Seal. About 1714 he was appointed, doubtless through the influence of this nobleman, to the office of Comptroller of the Customs at Kirkcaldy, having some years previously obtained that of Clerk to the Courts-martial and Councils of War for Scotland.

Smith's mother was a Miss Douglas, daughter of a Mr. Douglas, of Strathenry, a place lying a few miles away from Kirkcaldy. According to Dugald Stewart, she was a most affectionate and indulgent parent, so much so that it was only the excellence of the disposition of her boy that prevented him from being spoiled. Be that as it may, he proved to be in his turn an admirable son throughout the whole of the long period of sixty years for which she survived her husband.

The only incident which is recorded of Smith's childhood is that he once was stolen by tinkers from the door of his grandfather's house at Strathenry. Fortunately his grandfather conjectured what might have become of him, and, after a vigorous pursuit, discovered and rescued his grandson in a wood some miles off.

The boy was sent to the school kept by Mr. David Miller, in Kirkcaldy. He was then remarkable, not merely for love of reading and an extraordinary memory, but for a precocious absence of mind, and a habit, which in after years became at times startling to the bystanders, of speaking to himself. When he was

fourteen years old, he was sent, in accordance with the
not uncommon Scotch practice of those times, to the
university, that selected for him being Glasgow. At
Glasgow he gave himself up to Mathematics and Natural
Philosophy, and in 1840 obtained a "Snell" exhibition.
Snell was a merchant who, in the latter part of the seventeenth century, founded certain exhibitions in Glasgow
University, with the object of enabling deserving students
to go, for the purposes of study, to Balliol College,
Oxford. To Oxford accordingly Adam Smith went, a circumstance which distinguished his education from that
of the majority of his countrymen, including his friend
David Hume. At Oxford he remained for over six
years. According to Professor Thorold Rogers he seems
to have lived economically, the cost of his first quarter's
residence having been £7 5s. Even at a Scotch
university it would not be easy now-a-days to live at a
much less rate.

Oxford was at this time one of the last places to be
chosen as the educational nursery for a man who was to
break away from the traditions of the old political
economy, and effect a revolution in its principles. The
whole place was weighed down by intellectual listlessness,
and by indifference to the rapid movements of the time.
The pressure of the pent-up lava which was to break out
upon the world through France as its place of exit, was
unfelt in the English universities. But Smith's genius
was independent of its surroundings. Its bent was not
to be influenced by other minds. He appears from the
first to have busied himself with the study of ancient and
modern literature, a study the results of which his marvel-

lous memory enabled him to carry with him to the last.

His original intention had been to enter the Church. But his experience at Oxford, and in all probability the effect upon his mind of Hume's "Treatise," which appeared in the year before he went there, determined him definitely to abandon all thoughts of orders, and to take his chance of earning a livelihood by literature. To Scotland he returned in this frame of mind at the age of twenty-three. After a couple of years spent at Kirkcaldy, he removed to Edinburgh in the year 1748, and there, under the patronage of Lord Kames, delivered public lectures on Rhetoric and Belles-lettres. It was at this period in his life that he began to form his most important friendships. Among the earliest of these was a friendship with one of the most accomplished men of the world of the time. Alexander Wedderburn, afterwards Lord High Chancellor of Great Britain, Baron Loughborough, and Earl of Rosslyn, is, of all the eminent statesmen of the end of last century who failed in the great things of life for want of morality, perhaps the most remarkable. The history of his career is a prolonged justification of the bitter saying of Junius, that there was something about him that treachery could not trust. But a yet more important friendship was that which reached its maturity apparently about 1752, the historical friendship of Adam Smith and David Hume. In this there was none of the combination by contrast of complementary qualities which often impresses us in such relationships. They were both men of singularly easy-going temperament. Each displayed strikingly destructive

intellectual tendencies in combination with a certain
conservatism of mental disposition. So similar were
their pursuits, that in the case of persons who understood
each other less there would have been real danger of a
rivalry not altogether stingless. But there is no trace, so
far as we are aware, of any interruption in a sympathy
and intercourse which ended only with the death of
Hume.

They lived, sometimes together and always in constant communication, for a quarter of a century. The
chief difference between them was the difference of the
directions which they respectively gave to the great
currents of thought in the world; the origins of these
directions lay very close together. Whether Hume
could have been but for Smith, we cannot now say;
but we know that, but for Hume, Smith could never
have been.

In 1751 Smith was elected to the Chair of Logic in
Glasgow University, a chair which, four years afterwards,
he exchanged for that of Moral Philosophy. In the
practice incident to the lectures delivered from that
position he effected a revolution. Instead of pursuing
the course followed by his predecessors, including
Hutcheson, under whom he had himself been a student,
he imparted to his lectures a highly concrete character.
His course was divided into four parts, the first of which
embraced Natural Theology; the second, Ethics; the
third, Jurisprudence in its general principles; and the
fourth, The Nature of Political Institutions. The second
part was published by him as " The Theory of Moral
Sentiments." The fourth became known to the entire

civilized world under the immortal form of "The Wealth of Nations." A Professor Millar of Glasgow, one of Smith's contemporaries, gives the following description of his delivery :—

"There was no situation in which the abilities of Mr. Smith appeared to greater advantage than in that of a professor. In delivering his lectures he trusted almost entirely to extemporary elocution. His manner, though not graceful, was plain and unaffected ; and, as he seemed to be always interested in the subject, he never failed to interest his hearers. Each discourse consisted commonly of several distinct propositions, which he successively endeavoured to prove and illustrate. These propositions, when announced in general terms, had, from their extent, not infrequently, something of the air of a paradox. In his attempts to explain them, he often appeared at first not to be sufficiently possessed of the subject, and spoke with some hesitation. As he advanced, however, the matter seemed to crowd upon him, his manner became warm and animated, and his expression easy and fluent. In points susceptible of controversy, you could easily discern that he secretly conceived an opposition to his opinions, and that he was led, upon this account, to support them with greater energy and vehemence. By the fulness and variety of his illustrations, the subject gradually swelled in his hands, and acquired a dimension which, without a tedious repetition of the same views, was calculated to seize the attention of his audience; and to afford them pleasure as well as instruction in following the same object through all the diversity of shades and aspects in which it was presented, and afterwards in tracing it backwards to that original proposition or general truth from which this beautiful train of speculation had proceeded.

" His reputation as a professor was accordingly raised very high, and a multitude of students from a great distance resorted to the university, merely upon his account. These branches of science which he taught became fashionable at this place, and his opinions were the chief topics of discussion in clubs and literary societies. Even the small peculiarities in his pronunciation or manner of speaking became frequently the objects of imitation."

Ponderous though the excellent professor's description is, we can recognize in it a certain ring of truth. The reference to the copiousness of the lecturer's style recalls the diffuseness of " The Wealth of Nations." Smith was great in illustration, and, like many great masters of concrete statement, deficient in the power of arrangement. But to gain anything like an adequate impression of his personality, it is necessary to turn to the pages of a more capable observer than Professor Millar. In his Autobiography, Alexander Carlyle, the minister of Inveresk, one of the leaders of the Moderate party in the General Assembly, and one of the acutest worldly men of his time in Scotland, describes Smith thus :—

" Adam Smith, though perhaps only second to Hume in learning and ingenuity, was far inferior to him in

conversational talents. In that of public speaking they
were equal—David never tried it, and I never heard
Adam but once, which was at the first meeting of the
Select Society, when he opened up the design of the
meeting. His voice was harsh and his enunciation thick,
amounting almost to stammering. His conversation was
not colloquial, but like lecturing, in which I have been
told he was not deficient, especially when he grew warm.
He was the most absent man in company that I ever
saw—moving his lips, and talking to himself, and smiling
in the midst of large companies. If you awaked him
from his reverie, and made him attend to the subject
of the conversation, he immediately began a harangue,
and never stopped till he told you all he knew about it,
and with the utmost philosophical ingenuity. He knew
nothing of characters, and yet was ready to draw them on
the slightest invitation. But when you checked him or
doubted, he retracted with the utmost ease, and contra-
dicted all he had been saying. His journey abroad with
the Duke of Buccleuch cured him in part of these foibles;
but still he appeared very unfit for the intercourse of the
world as a travelling tutor. But the duke was a character
both in point of heart and understanding to surmount
all disadvantages—he could learn nothing ill from a
philosopher of the utmost probity and benevolence. If
he (Smith) had been a man of address and the world, he
might, perhaps, have given a ply to the duke's fine mind,
which was much better when left to its own energy.
Charles Townsend had chosen Smith, not for his fitness
for the purpose, but for his own glory in having sent an
eminent Scottish philosopher to travel with the duke."

The duke here alluded to, with no little indication of partiality, was the Duke of Buccleuch. We shall see presently under what circumstances Smith became his tutor. As regards the absence of mind, Dr. Carlyle most likely had present to him when he wrote a story which went the round at the time. Smith had been invited to Dalkeith Palace to meet an eminent statesman who was staying there. During, or after dinner, he fell into a reverie, and began to discourse aloud upon the merits, or rather demerits, of this very politician, in language which was neither guarded nor indirect. On being recalled to consciousness of his surroundings, he was so covered with confusion that he again relapsed into reverie, muttering to himself and to the company, as the reflection of his inner mind—"Deil care, deil care, it's all true!"

Notwithstanding that his academic home was Glasgow, Smith appears to have lived a great deal in Edinburgh at this time. He was a prominent member of the famous Poker Club, which had its origin in an association formed in Edinburgh for the purpose of protesting and agitating against the indisposition of the Government to extend the Militia system to Scotland, an indisposition which was doubtless due to the fear of Jacobitism, and a very vivid recollection of Culloden. This club was dissolved in disgust at the resolution of the authorities to levy a heavy duty on its favourite beverage—claret; and in its place there was established a debating society known as the "Select," the first meeting of which took place on May 1, 1754.

The Select Society reckoned among its members most

of the literary notabilities of the Edinburgh of that day. Besides Smith and his friend Hume, it included Home, the author of "Douglas," Dr. Hugh Blair, Sir David Dalrymple, Dr. Robertson of Gladsmuir, and a score of other well-known men. It is remarkable that the question fixed on for discussion at the second meeting was the advantage of bounties on the exportation of corn, and that the debate was to be opened by Smith himself. It is clear that at this time the attention of both Smith and his friend Hume was closely concentrated on the question of the validity of the Mercantile System.

One well-known epigram—the work of Home—survives to us as a reminiscence of these old Edinburgh days. Before the levy of prohibitive duties on claret, which had led to the dissolution of the Poker Club, this wine had been imported into Scotland under the title of "Southampton port," paying only certain small duties. It was consumed at this time in Scotland in quantities the enormous magnitude of which can only be realized after reading detailed descriptions of the ways and customs of the then generation. The blow to the consumers, and the privations which they suffered through the change in the law, were summed up by Home—

> "Firm and erect the Caledonian stood,
>   Old was his mutton, and his claret good ;
>   Let him drink port, the English statesmen cried ;
>   He drank the poison, and his spirit died."

It has already been mentioned that Smith occupied the Chair of Logic in Glasgow, before his appointment to that of Moral Philosophy. There is evidence, in the form of a letter from Hume to Dr. Cullen, that Hume himself was anxious to be appointed to the Chair of Logic, rendered vacant by his friend's change of position. Some of the electors seem to have taken steps to promote the choice of no less a personage than Burke. But in these days the spirit of lion-hunting, if it prevailed at all, prevailed only in regard to persons of social distinction; and the wholesome disinclination of the general public to confide the education of the coming generation to individuals whose opinions it did not understand, led to the choice of neither Burke nor Hume, but a certain Mr. Clow.

In 1759 appeared " The Theory of Moral Sentiments." As sometimes happens, the author seems to have exhansted his interest in his work in the course of its creation, and it is recorded that from the day of its publication his attention became increasingly concentrated upon economical subjects. In the course of the four years during which he continued at Glasgow after 1759, his lectures became more and more devoted to Jurisprudence and Political Economy. On the whole, however, the book proved a success, although it was not destined to become a substantial, or indeed any part, of the foundation upon which its author's fame now reposes. His great fault as a thinker on morals is the absence, in his case, of any metaphysical training. It was Hume who first made it plain that Metaphysics and Ethics are inextricably intertwined; and since his time the tendency of modern thought has been to regard them as altogether mutually dependent.

The following letter from Hume to his friend on the occasion of the appearance of the book, is worth quoting at length :—

"DEAR SIR,—I give you thanks for the agreeable present of your theory. Wedderburn and I made presents of our own copies to such of our acquaintances as we thought good judges, and proper to spread the reputation of the book. I sent one to the Duke of Argyle, to Lord Lyttelton, Horace Walpole, Soame Jenyns, and Burke, an Irish gentleman, who wrote lately a very pretty treatise on the Sublime. Millar desired my permission to send one in your name to Dr. Warburton.

"I have delayed writing to you till I could tell you something of the success of the book, and could prognosticate, with some probability, whether it should be finally damned to oblivion, or should be registered in the temple of immortality. Though it has been published only a few weeks, I think there appear already such strong symptoms that I can almost venture to foretell its fate. It is, in short, this——

"But I have been interrupted in my letter by a foolish, impertinent visit of one who has lately come from Scotland. He tells me that the University of Glasgow intend to declare Rouet's office vacant upon his going abroad with Lord Hope. I question not but you will have our friend Ferguson in your eye, in case another project for procuring him a place in the University of Edinburgh should fail. Ferguson has very much polished and improved his treatise on Refinement, and, with some amendments, it will make an admirable book, and

discovers an elegant and a singular genius. The Epi-
goniad I hope will do, but it is somewhat uphill work.
As I doubt not but you consult the Reviews sometimes
at present, you will see, in *The Critical Review*, a letter
upon that poem, and I desire you to employ your con-
jectures in finding out the author. Let me see a sample
of your skill in knowing hands by your guessing at the
person.

"I am afraid of Kames' 'Law Tracts.' A man might
as well think of making a fine sauce by a mixture of
wormwood and aloes, as an agreeable composition by
joining metaphysics and Scottish law. However, the
book, I believe, has merit, though few people will take
the pains of inquiring into it. But to return to your
book and its success in this town. I must tell you——

"A plague of interruptions! I ordered myself to be
denied, and yet here is one that has broke in upon me
again. He is a man of letters, and we have had a good
deal of literary conversation. You told me that you was
curious of literary anecdotes, and therefore I shall inform
you of a few that have come to my knowledge. I believe
that I have mentioned to you already Helvetius's book
'De l'Esprit.' It is worth your reading; not for its philosophy, which I do not highly value, but for its agreeable
composition. I had a letter from him a few days ago,
wherein he tells me that my name was much oftener in
the manuscript, but that the censor of books at Paris
obliged him to strike it out.

"Voltaire has lately published a small work called
'Candide; ou, L'Optimisme.' I shall give you a detail
of it. But what is all this to my book? say you. My

dear Mr. Smith, have patience: compose yourself to tranquility; show yourself a philosopher in practice as well as in profession: think on the emptiness, and rashness, and futility of the common judgments of men, how little they are regulated by reason in any subject, much more in philosophical subjects, which so far exceed the comprehension of the vulgar.

> ‘Non si quid turbida Roma
> Elevet, accedas : examenve improbum in illâ
> Castiges trutinâ : nec te quæsiveris extra.’

A wise man's kingdom is his own breast, or, if he ever looks farther, it will only be to the judgment of a select few who are free from prejudices, and capable of examining his work. Nothing indeed can be a stronger presumption of falsehood than the approbation of the multitude, and Phocion, you know, always suspected himself of some blunder when he was attended with the applauses of the populace.

"Supposing, therefore, that you have duly prepared yourself for the worst by all these reflections, I proceed to tell you the melancholy news that your book has been very unfortunate, for the public seem disposed to applaud it extremely. It was looked for by the foolish people with some impatience, and the mob of literati are beginning already to be very loud in its praises. Three bishops called yesterday at Millar's shop in order to buy copies, and to ask questions about the author. The Bishop of Peterborough said he had passed the evening in a company where he heard it extolled above all books in the world. The Duke of Argyle is more decisive than he uses to be in its favour. I suppose he either considers it an exotic, or thinks the author will be serviceable to him in the Glasgow elections. Lord Lyttelton says that Robertson, and Smith, and Bower are the glories of English literature. Oswald protests he does not know whether he has reaped more instruction or entertainment from it. But you may easily judge what reliance can be put on his judgment who has been engaged all his life in public business, and who never sees any faults in his friends. Millar exults, and brags that two-thirds of the edition are already sold, and that he is now sure of success. You see what a son of the earth that is, to value books only by the profit they bring him. In that view I believe it may prove a very good book.

"Charles Townsend, who passes for the cleverest fellow in England, is so taken with the performance that he said to Oswald he would put the Duke of Buccleuch under the author's care, and would make it worth his while to accept of that charge. As soon as I heard of this I called on him twice, with a view of talking with him about the matter, and convincing him of the propriety of sending that young nobleman to Glasgow; for I could not hope that he could offer you any terms which would tempt you to renounce your professorship; but I missed him. Mr. Townsend passes for being a little uncertain in his resolutions, so, perhaps, you need not build much on his sally.

"In recompense for so many mortifying things, which nothing but truth could have extorted from me, and which I could easily have multiplied to a greater number, I doubt not but you are so good a Christian as to return good for evil, and to flatter my vanity by telling me that all the godly in Scotland abuse me for my account of John Knox and the Reformation. I suppose you are glad to see my paper end, and that I am obliged to conclude with—Your humble servant."

In those days men of letters had time to impart form to their correspondence.

Charles Townsend, to whose promise Hume refers with some doubt in the letter just quoted, proved as good as his word, although some time elapsed before his intention was carried into effect. In 1763 Smith received from him an invitation to travel in Europe with the Duke of Buccleuch, accompanied by an offer of terms and opportunities so tempting that the professor was induced to resign his chair, and enter upon a (to him) entirely new phase of life.

The duke and his distinguished fellow traveller proceeded to Paris, where, however, they remained only a few days, in the first instance, returning later on. From here the latter sent a formal letter of resignation of his chair to Glasgow, the reception of which was recorded in the university records in the following terms :—

"The meeting accepts of Dr. Smith's resignation in terms of the above letter," (one from Smith, in which he expressed a wish that whoever was his successor might not only do credit to the office by his abilities, but be a comfort to the very excellent men with whom he was likely to spend his life, by the probity of his heart, and the goodness of his temper), "and the office of Professor of Moral Philosophy in this university is therefore declared vacant. The university, at the same time, cannot help expressing their sincere regret at the removal of Dr. Smith, whose distinguished probity and amiable qualities procured him the esteem and affection of his colleagues; and whose uncommon genius, great abilities, and extensive learning, did so much honour to this society; his elegant and ingenious 'Theory of Moral Sentiments' having recommended him to the esteem of men of taste and literature throughout Europe. His happy talent in illustrating abstracted subjects, and faithful assiduity in communicating useful knowledge, distinguished him as a professor, and at once afforded the greatest pleasure and the most important instruction to the youth under his care."

That Smith's life in Paris was not at first entirely to his mind, the following extract from a letter to Hume shows unmistakably :—

"The duke is acquainted with no Frenchman whatever. I cannot cultivate the acquaintance of the few with whom I am acquainted, as I cannot bring them to our house and am not always at liberty to go to theirs. The life which I led at Glasgow was a pleasurable dissipated life in comparison of that which I lead here at present. I have begun to write a book in order to pass away the time. You may believe I have very little to do. If Sir James would come and spend a month with us in his travels it would not only be a great satisfaction to me, but he might by his influence and example be of great service to the duke."

Matters however improved as time went on, and in the end the visit to Paris proved as great a success, as it threatened to be a failure.

From Paris the travellers went on to Toulouse, where they remained for eighteen months, and from Toulouse, through the South of France, by Geneva to Paris (where they must have arrived at Christmas, 1765), and in Paris they remained until the following October. Smith had been provided with introductions from Hume, and these, together with facilities which he obtained in virtue of his charge, brought him into some of the best company in the city. Turgot, Quesnay, Necker, D'Alembert, Helvetius, and the Abbé Morellet were among the acquaintances of this period of his life. Two of these names belong to men who made a profound and lasting impression on his mind.

The influence of Turgot and Quesnay had probably more to do with the opinions which were afterwards elaborated into a systematic form in "The Wealth of Nations," than any of their other antecedents. How great was Smith's admiration of Quesnay, notwithstanding that the "Agricultural System" of that thinker was one of the two great fallacies which "The Wealth of Nations" was written to expose, will be seen at a glance by any one who looks at the ninth chapter of the fourth book of that work. The tour in France was for Smith, and presumably for his companion, a most successful one. In the duke's own words : " In October, 1766, we returned to London, after having spent near three years together, without the slightest disagreement or coolness ;—on my part with every advantage that could be expected from the society of such a man. We continued to live in friendship till the hour of his death; and I shall always remain with the impression of having lost a friend whom I loved and respected, not only for his great talents, but for every private virtue." There can be no doubt that during his stay in France, Smith laid the foundations, not only of an immense stock of illustrations of economical principles but also of an extensive acquaintance with French literature. His progress in the language appears, however, if we may trust the Abbé Morellet to have been less satisfactory : " Il parloit fort mal notre langue, mais nous parlâmes théorie commerciale, banque, Crédit public," &c. ("He spoke French very badly, but we discussed the theory of commerce, banks, public credit," &c.)

On his return to this country, he went, almost at once, into a retirement at Kirkcaldy from which he did not emerge for ten years. His friends were aware that he was engrossed by the composition of some great book, but the following extract from a letter, dated in 1772, suggests that even Hume had not been taken fully into his confidence on the subject : " I shall not take any excuse from your state of health, which I suppose only a subterfuge invented by indolence and love of solitude. Indeed, my dear Smith, if you continue to hearken to complaints of this nature, you will cut yourself out entirely from human society, to the great loss of both parties." In a still earlier letter, however, written from his house in James's Court (which commanded a view of the Firth of Forth and of Kirkcaldy on the opposite side), Hume refers to the general character of his friend's occupation :—

"DEAR SMITH,—I am glad to have come within sight of you, and to have a view of Kirkaldy from my windows, but as I wish also to be within speaking terms of you I wish we could concert measures for that purpose. I am mortally sick at sea, and regard with horror and a kind of hydrophobia the great gulf that lies between us. I am also tired of travelling as much as you ought naturally to be of staying at home. I therefore propose to you to come hither and pass some days with me in this solitude. I want to know what you have been doing, and propose to exact a rigorous account of the method in which you have employed yourself during your retreat. I am positive you are in the wrong in many of your speculations, especially where you have the misfortune to differ from me. All these are reasons for our meeting, and I wish you would make me some reasonable proposal for that purpose. There is no habitation on the island of Inchkeith, otherwise I should challenge you to meet me on that spot, and neither of us ever to leave the place till we were fully agreed on all points of controversy. I expect General Conway here to-morrow whom I shall attend to Roseneath, and I shall remain there a few days. On my return I expect to find a letter from you, containing a bold acceptance of this defiance.—I am, dear Smith, yours sincerely."

His house at Kirkcaldy, which Smith inhabited along with his brother and his cousin, Miss Douglas, was exactly suited for his purpose. It was sufficiently near Edinburgh to enable him to get there easily by a sail across the Firth of Forth, and it was yet a place where he was secure from too frequent interruption by his friends. The town was a manufacturing one, and he could consequently obtain information at first hand on commercial topics. Besides this, it afforded him a small circle of quiet acquaintances, in whose society it was his habit to relax, though sparingly, from his labours. At last in 1776, early in the year, there appeared, in two quarto volumes, the first edition of the "Inquiry into the Nature and Causes of the Wealth of Nations." Hume, who was now in a dying condition, wrote to congratulate the author in a characteristic letter :—

"EDINBURGH, *April* 1, 1776.

"EUGE! BELLE! DEAR MR. SMITH,—I am much pleased with your performance, and the perusal of it has taken me from a state of great anxiety. It was a work of so much expectation, by yourself, by your friends, and by the public, that I trembled for its appearance, but am now much relieved. Not but that the reading of it necessarily requires so much attention, and the public is disposed to give so little, that I shall still doubt for some time of its being at first very popular. But it has depth, and solidity, and acuteness, and is so much illustrated by curious facts, that it must at last take the public attention. It is probably much improved by your last abode in London. If you were here at my fireside, I should dispute some of your principles. I cannot think that the rent of farms makes any part of the price of the produce, but that the price is determined altogether by the quantity and the demand. It appears to me impossible that the king of France can take a seignorage of 8 per cent. upon the coinage. Nobody would bring bullion to the mint. It would be all sent to Holland or England, where it might be coined and sent back to France, for less than 2 per cent. Accordingly, Necker says that the French king takes only 2 per cent. of seignorage. But these and a hundred other points are fit only to be discussed in conversation. I hope it will be soon, for I am in a very bad state of health and cannot afford a long delay. I fancy you are acquainted with Mr. Gibbon. I like his performance extremely, and have ventured to tell him, had I not been personally acquainted with him, I should never have expected such an excellent work from the pen of an Englishman. It is lamentable to consider how much that nation has declined in literature during our time. I hope he did not take amiss the national reflection.

"All your friends here are in great grief at present for the death of Baron Mure, which is an irreparable loss to our society. He was among the oldest and best friends I had in the world."

Before passing to the story of the great success of Adam Smith's life, the effect of his book upon the contemporary world, we may pause to notice a more questionable incident in his history. Of all the qualities, of an extrinsic nature, which the character of a great man ought to display, moral courage is probably the one which the public, perhaps rightly, appreciates most. There is ground for supposing that throughout his career Smith was never very frank about his theological opinions. · What these were we do not know. There is no record (that the writer of these memoirs has been able to discover) of Smith's lectures in Glasgow, so far as these topics are concerned. But the traditions which survive, and the internal evidence afforded by his writings, point to the apparent similarity of his views to those of Hume. It is, in any view, far from admirable that he should have hesitated to peril his reputation and interests, whatever these might amount to, in the way he did, for the sake of his friend. That he did hesitate, Hume's letters to him show—

" LONDON, *May* 3, 1776.

"My DEAR FRIEND,—I send you enclosed an ostensible letter, conformably to your desire. I think, however, your scruples groundless. Was Mallet any wise hurt by his publication of Lord Bolingbroke? He received an office afterwards from the present king and Lord Bute, the most prudish men in the world, and he always justifies himself by his sacred regard to the will of a dead friend. At the same time I own that your scruples have a specious appearance. But my opinion is that if upon my death you determine never to publish these papers, you should leave them sealed up with my brother and family, with some inscription that you reserve to yourself the power of reclaiming them whenever you think proper. If I live a few years longer I publish them myself. I consider an observation of Rochefoucault that a wind though it extinguishes a candle blows up a fire.

"You may be surprised to hear me talk of living years, considering the state you saw me in, and the sentiments which both I and all my friends at Edinburgh entertained on that subject. But though I cannot come up entirely to the sanguine notions of our friend John, I find myself very much recovered on the road, and I hope Bath waters and farther journeys may effect my cure.

"By the little company I have seen I find the town very full of your book which meets with general approbation. Many people think particular parts disputable, but this you certainly expected. I am glad that I am one of the number, as these parts will be the subject of future conversation between us. I set out for Bath, I believe on Monday, by Sir John Pringle's directions who says that he sees nothing to be apprehended in my case. If you write to me (hem! hem l), I say if you write to me, send your letter under cover to Mr. Strahan who will have my direction."

LONDON, *May* 3, 1776.

"MY DEAR SIR,—After reflecting more maturely on that article of my will by which I left you the disposal of all my papers with a request that you should publish my 'Dialogues concerning Natural Religion,' I have become sensible that both on account of the nature of the work, and of your situation, it may be improper to hurry on that publication. I therefore take the present opportunity of qualifying that friendly bequest. I am content to leave it entirely to your discretion at what time you will publish that piece, or whether you will publish it at all.

"You will find among my papers a very inoffensive piece called 'My own Life," which I composed a few days before I left Edinburgh, when I thought, as did all my friends, that my life was despaired of. There can be no objection that the small piece should be sent to Messrs. Strahan and Cadell, and the proprietors of my other works, to be prefixed to any future edition of them."

Hume soon saw that Smith would not undertake the trust he sought to commit to him. He did not absolutely decline to edit the "Dialogues concerning Natural Religion," but it became plain that he was most unwilling to do so. It may be said that this unwillingness was as much in the interests of Hume's own memory, as of his own reputation, and this is the best excuse that can be made for him. At all events, Hume determined to revoke, and did revoke, the direction by a codicil to his will, and entrusted the task to Strahan, the publisher. To the latter Smith wrote, after Hume's death, thus—

"I once had persuaded him to leave it entirely to my discretion either to publish them at what time I thought proper, or not to publish them at all. Had he continued of this mind, the manuscript would have been most carefully preserved, and upon my decease restored to his family; but it should never have been published in my lifetime. When you have read it, you will perhaps consult some prudent friend about what you ought to do."

The book was ultimately published, not by Strahan, whom Smith appears to have terrified, but by Hume's nephew, in 1779.

No life of Adam Smith can be complete without some account of his description of the death-bed of his friend. That description was contained in a letter which, though somewhat long, relates to a matter of such interest that it is worth quoting at length. It is a description which refutes completely the nursery tales upon the subject which were set abroad at the time, and for long passed current. Fortunately we live in a generation which countenances malicious gossip on such a topic but little.

"KIRKALDY, FIFESHIRE, *Nov.* 9, 1776.

"DEAR SIR,—It is with a real, though a very melancholy pleasure, that I sit down to give you some account of the behaviour of our excellent friend, Mr. Hume, during his last illness.

"Though, in his own judgment, his disease was mortal and incurable, yet he allowed himself to be prevailed upon, by the entreaty of his friends, to try what might be the effects of a long journey. A few days before he set out he wrote that account of his own life, which, together with his other papers, he has left to your care. My account, therefore, shall begin where his ends.

"He set out for London towards the end of April, and at Morpeth met with **Mr.** John Home and myself, who had both come down from London on purpose to see him, expecting to have found him at Edinburgh. Mr. Home returned with him, and attended him during the whole of his stay in England, with that care and attention which might be expected from a temper so perfectly friendly and affectionate. As I had written to my mother that she might expect me in Scotland, I was under the necessity of continuing my journey. His disease seemed to yield to exercise and change of air, and when he arrived in London he was apparently in much better health than when he left Edinburgh. He was advised to go to Bath to drink the waters, which appeared for some time to have so good an effect upon him that even he himself began to entertain, what he was not apt to do, a better opinion of his own health. His symptoms, however, soon returned with their usual violence, and from that moment he gave up all thoughts of recovery, but submitted with the utmost cheerfulness, and the most perfect complacency and resignation. Upon his return to Edinburgh, though he found himself much weaker, yet his cheerfulness never abated, and he continued to divert himself as usual, with correcting his own works for a new edition, and reading books of amusement, with the conversation of his friends, and, sometimes in the evening, with a party at his favourite game of whist. His cheerfulness was so great, his conversation and amusements run so much in their usual strain that, notwithstanding all bad symptoms, many people could not believe he was dying. 'I shall tell your friend, Colonel Edmondstone,' said Doctor Dundas to him one day, 'that I left you much better, and in a fair way **of** recovery.' 'Doctor,' said he, 'as I believe you would not choose to tell anything but the truth, you had better tell him, that I am dying as fast as my enemies, if I have any, could wish, and as easily and as cheerfully as my best friends could desire.'   Colonel Edmondstone soon afterwards came to see him, and took leave of him ; and on his way home he could not forbear writing him a letter bidding him once more an eternal adieu, and applying to him, as a dying man, the beautiful French verses in which the Abbé Chaulieu, in expectation of his own death, laments his approaching separation from his friend, the Marquis de la Fare.   Mr. Hume's magnanimity and firmness were such, that his most affectionate friends knew that they hazarded nothing in talking or writing to him as to a dying man, and that, so far from being hurt by this frankness, he was rather pleased and flattered by it.   I happened to come into his room while he was reading this letter, which he had just received, and which he immediately showed me.   I told him that though I was sensible how very much he was weakened, and that appearances were in many respects very bad, yet his cheerfulness was still so great, the spirit of life seemed still to be so very strong in him, that I could not help entertaining some faint hopes.   He answered—'Your hopes are groundless.   An habitual diarrhœa of more than a year's standing would be a very bad disease at any age : at my age it is a mortal one.   When I lie down in the evening, I feel myself weaker than when I rose in the morning ; and when I rise in the morning, weaker than when I lay down in the evening. I am sensible, besides, that some of my vital parts are affected, so that I must soon die.' 'Well,' said I, 'if it must be so, you have at least the satisfaction of leaving all your friends, your brother's family in particular, in great prosperity.' He said that he felt that satisfaction so sensibly, that when he was reading a few days before, Lucian's 'Dialogues of the Dead,' among all the excuses which are alleged to Charon for not entering readily into his boat, he could not find one that fitted him: he had no house to finish, he had no daughter to provide for, he had no enemies upon whom he wished to revenge himself. 'I could not well imagine,' said he, 'what excuse I could make to Charon in order to obtain a little delay. I have done everything of cousequence which I ever meant to do; and I could at no time expect to leave my relations and friends in a better situation than that in which I am now like to leave them: I therefore have all reason to die contented.' He then diverted himself with inventing several jocular excuses, which he supposed he might make to Charon, and with imagining the very surly answers which it might suit the character of Charon to return to them. 'Upon further consideration,' said he, 'I thought I might say to him, good Charon, I have been correcting my works for a new edition; allow me a little time that I may see how the public receives the alterations.' But Charon would answer, ' When you have seen the effect of these, you will be for making other alterations. There will be no end of such excuses; so, honest friend, please step into the boat.' But I might still urge, 'Have a little patience, good Charon; I have been endeavouring to open the eyes of the public. If I live a few years longer, I may have the satisfaction of seeing the downfall of some of the prevailing systems of superstition.' But Charon would then lose all temper and decency. 'You loitering rogue; that will not happen these many hundred years. Do you fancy I will grant you a lease for so long a term? Get into the boat this instant, you lazy, loitering rogue.'

"But though Mr. Hume always talked of his approaching dissolution with great cheerfulness, he never affected to make any parade of his magnanimity. He never mentioned the subject but when the conversation naturally led to it, and never dwelt longer upon it than the course of the conversation happened to require: it was a subject, indeed, which occurred pretty frequently, in consequence of the inquiries which his friends, who came to see him, naturally made concerning the state of his health. The conversation which I mentioned above, and which passed on Thursday the 8th of August, was the last, except one, that I ever had with him. He had now become so very weak, that the company of his most intimate friends fatigued him; for his cheerfulness was still so great, his complaisance and social disposition were still so entire, that when any friend was with him he could not help talking more, and with greater exertion than suited the weakness of his body. At his own desire, therefore, I agreed to leave Edinburgh, where I was staying partly upon his account, and returned to my mother's house here, at Kirkaldy, upon condition that he would send for me whenever he wished to see me; the physician who saw him most frequently, Dr. Black, undertaking in the meantime, to write me occasionally an account of the state of his health.

"On the 22nd of August, the doctor wrote me the following letter :—

"'Since my last Mr. Hume has passed his time pretty easily, but is much weaker. He sits up, goes downstairs once a day, and amuses himself with reading, but seldom sees anybody. He finds that even the conversation of his most intimate friends fatigues and oppresses him; and it is happy that he does not need it, for he is quite free from anxiety, impatience, or low spirits, and passes his time very well with the assistance of amusing books.'

"I received the day after a letter from Mr. Hume himself, of which the following is an extract :—

"'EDINBURGH, *August* 23, 1776.

"'MY DEAREST FRIEND,—I am obliged to make use of my nephew's hand in writing to you, as I do not rise to-day.

*   *   *   *   *   *

"'I go very fast to decline, and last night had a small fever, which I hoped might put a quicker period to this tedious illness; but unluckily it has, in a great measure, gone off. I cannot submit to your coming over here on my account, as it is possible for me to see you so small a part of the day, but Dr. Black can better inform you concerning the degree of strength which may from time to time remain with me. Adieu, etc.'

"Three days after I received the following letter from Dr. Black :—

"'EDINBURGH, *August* 26, 1776.

"'DEAR SIR,—Yesterday, about four o'clock afternoon, Mr. Hume expired. The near approach of his death became evident in the night between Thursday and Friday, when his disease became excessive, and soon weakened him so much that he could no longer rise out of his bed. He continued to the last perfectly sensible, and free from much pain or feeling of distress. He never dropped the smallest expression of impatience ; but when he had occasion to speak to the people about him, always did it with affection and tenderness. I thought it improper to write to bring you over, especially as I heard that he had dictated a letter to you desiring you not to come. When he became very weak it cost him an effort to speak, and he died in such a happy composure of mind, that nothing could exceed it !'

"Thus died our most excellent and never-to-be-forgotten friend, concerning whose philosophical opinions men will, no doubt, judge variously, every one approving or condemning them according as they happen to coincide or disagree with his own; but concerning whose character and conduct there can scarce be a difference of opinion. His temper, indeed, seemed to be more happily balanced —if I may be allowed such an expression—than that perhaps of any other man I have ever known. Even in the lowest state of his fortune, his great and necessary frugality never hindered him from exercising, upon

proper occasions, acts both of charity and generosity.
It was a frugality, founded not upon avarice, but upon
the love of independency. The extreme gentleness of
his nature never weakened either the firmness of his mind
or the steadiness of his resolutions. His constant plea-
santry was the genuine effusion of good-nature and good-
humour tempered with delicacy and modesty, and without
even the slightest tincture of malignity—so frequently the
disagreeable source of what is called wit in other men.
It never was the meaning of his raillery to mortify, and
therefore, far from offending, it seldom failed to please
and delight even those who were the object of it. To
his friends—who were frequently the object of it—there
was not perhaps any one of all his great and amiable
qualities, which contributed more to endear his conversation. And that gaiety of temper so agreeable in society,
but which is so often accompanied with frivolous and
superficial qualities, was in him certainly attended with
the most severe application, the most extensive learning,
the greatest depth of thought, and a capacity in every
respect the most comprehensive. Upon the whole, I
have always considered him, both in his lifetime and since
his death, as approaching as nearly to the idea of a
perfectly wise and virtuous man, as perhaps the nature
of human frailty will permit.

" I ever am, dear sir, most affectionately yours,

"ADAM SMITH."

Hume died, as he had lived, a brave, upright man ;
and it is some satisfaction to know that his moral, as well
as his mental qualities, remained intact until the last.

The less tolerant section of the public, no doubt, expected at the time to find that his death-bed was a scene of mental anguish, for reasons as good as those which prompted its less educated members to crowd round his grave in the Calton burying-ground, in the anticipation of seeing his body snatched from its last resting-place in a blue flame.

With Hume's death there came a great change over the life and habits of his friend. It was not merely that old associations, and the tie which bound him to Edinburgh, were broken. In a few months he had become famous. Hitherto he had been known only as a man of letters, who had written a book of some merit upon Moral Philosophy, and whose greatest distinction was his association with Hume. But now he had, almost at a stroke, kindled an opposition fiercer and more substantial than any which Hume had raised. There are comparatively few men who become excited at an attack on their faith. There are many who resent, with the utmost conceivable bitterness, an attack upon their pockets. Were the principles of " The Wealth of Nations " to be adopted, the whole of the then business of the mercantile community must be upset. The promulgation of a far less heretical doctrine cost Burke his seat at Bristol, and even to-day, when the teaching of Adam Smith has become familiar to us, and his principles have long since been made part of the law of the land, it is over the issues which he placed before the world that the political controversy rages most keenly. As soon as the practical bearing of the book became understood, a storm of criticism arose around it. Statesmen and men of letters alike were at once interested in it, and unlike "The Treatise of Human Nature," it produced its effect almost at once. The enthusiasm with which this author was received by politicians of the first rank may be gathered from what took place on the occasion of a dinner-party to which Smith was invited by Lord Melville at Wimbledon, shortly after the appearance of the book. Pitt, Grenville, Addington, and several others were among the guests. Smith was late and apologized. The whole company rose, and Pitt exclaimed—"We will stand till you are seated, for we are all your scholars!"

In the midst of the storm which he had raised, Smith went to London. When he resigned his chair thirteen years previously, in order to travel with the Duke of Buccleuch, the trustees of his pupil had settled upon him an annuity of £300, a sum which was amply sufficient for his comparatively simple wants, and which enabled him to use his time as he pleased. He now plunged into the society which was only too glad to receive him. He became one of the little circle of famous men at whose social gatherings Sir Joshua Reynolds, Garrick, and Dr. Johnson presided. With all the members of this circle Smith did not get on equally well. There is, indeed, evidence in the pages of Boswell—who, by the way, had been a student under Smith at Glasgow—that Smith and Johnson, notwithstanding that they belonged to the same club, agreed at times very ill indeed. One scandalous story, however, related by Sir Walter Scott, whether or not it is wholly without foundation, is, on the face of it, inaccurate. On the authority of Professor Miller, Scott charges Boswell with having omitted to mention that

Smith and Johnson had met, not merely in London, but also in Glasgow in 1773, and that Smith, leaving the party where he had met the distinguished tourist, went on to another party where Miller was. Knowing that Smith had been in Johnson's society, the company were anxious to learn how they had got on. At first Smith, so the story goes, would only answer, " He's a brute— he's a brute ! " but on further inquiry it appeared that Johnson no sooner saw Smith, than he attacked him for some point of his famous letter to Strahan on the death of Hume. Smith vindicated the truth of his statement. "What did Johnson say ? " was the universal inquiry. "Why, he said," replied Smith, with the deepest impression of resentment, " He said— *You lie !* " "And what did you reply ? " "I said—You are a son of a —— ! " It is sufficient comment on the credibility of this story to point out that while Johnson's visit to Glasgow took place in 1773, Hume did not die until 1776.

After remaining for two years in London, and mixing while there with the most brilliant literary society of the period, Smith returned to Scotland, for which country he had been appointed, through the influence of his friend the Duke of Buccleuch, one of the Commissioners of Customs. The duties of this office required his presence in Edinburgh, and accordingly his mother, and his cousin, Miss Douglas, removed from Kirkcaldy, and joined him there. The household was only broken up by the deaths, of the former in 1784, and of the latter in 1788. He never got over his mother's death. For sixty years her house had been his real home.

Dugald Stewart relates, that there had once in Smith's

history been an attachment of a different kind. "In the
early part of Mr. Smith's life it is well known to his
friends that he was for several years attached to a young
lady of great beauty and accomplishment. How far his
addresses were favourably received, or what the circumstances were which prevented their union, I have not
been able to learn; but I believe it to be pretty certain
that after this disappointment he laid aside all thoughts
of marriage. The lady to whom I allude died also
unmarried. She survived Mr. Smith for a considerable
number of years, and was alive long after the publication
of the first edition of this memoir. I had the pleasure
of seeing her when she was turned of eighty, and when
she still retained evident traces of her former beauty.
The powers of her understanding and the gaiety of her
temper seemed to have suffered nothing from the hand of
time."

From 1778, when he came to Edinburgh, until his
death twelve years afterwards, Smith lived in a house
called Panmure House, at the bottom of a close, a little
way below the Canongate Church. There he was fond
of entertaining his friends in the most hospitable fashion.
He seems to have somewhat neglected the opportunity,
which the light duties of his office afforded him, of
revising and completing his various works. Indeed he
appears to have written nothing, and to have studied
little, if at all. It is recorded that he found the official
demands upon his time enough to waste his spirits and
dissipate his attention. But he went much into society,
and as both the drawing of his figure and the letterpress
in "Kay's Portraits" show, he was one of the prominen:

Edinburgh figures of his time. He was no great talker, so far as ordinary conversation was concerned. But when drawn out, or roused, he would pour forth a very torrent on all manner of topics upon which his vast reading and retentive memory furnished him with abundance of materials. Ordinarily, he shrank from public controversy. On one memorable occasion only do we hear of his being made the subject of anything approaching to a public attack. It was the publication of his famous letter to Strahan upon the death of Hume that called forth an anonymous epistle from " One of the people called Christians." The author of this composition turned out to be Dr. Horne, the Bishop of Norwich. His language was by no means conciliatory. Not unjustifiably conjecturing that there was considerable sympathy on the part of Smith with the peculiar tenets of his dead friend, the bishop writes after the frank fashion of those days :—

"You have been lately employed in embalming a philosopher; his *body*, I believe I must say, for concerning the other part of his nature neither you nor he seem to have entertained an idea, sleeping or waking. Else it surely might have claimed a little of your care and attention; and we would think the belief of the soul's existence and immortality could do no harm, if it did no good, in a Theory of Moral Sentiments. But every gentleman understands his own business best. . . . Are you sure, and can you make us sure, that there really exist no such things as God, a future state of rewards and punishments? If so, all is

well. Let us *then*, in our last hours, read Lucian, and
play at whist, and droll upon Charon and his boat; let
us die as foolish and insensible, as much like our brother
philosophers, the calves of the field and the asses of the
desert, as we can, for the life of us. . . . Upon the whole,
doctor, your meaning is good, but I think you will not
succeed this time. You would persuade us by the
example of David Hume, Esq., that Atheism is the only
cordial for low spirits, and the proper antidote against
the fear of death."

Smith wisely ignored this letter, and the controversy
which threatened, dropped.

Dugald Stewart has preserved to us some reminiscences
of Adam Smith's manner of composition. He composed
slowly and with difficulty throughout, unlike Hume, who
latterly acquired a facility so great that the last volumes of
his " History " were printed from his original copy with a
few marginal corrections. Smith's practice when com-
posing was to walk up and down his room dictating to a
secretary. With some parts of what he had done he
was never satisfied. He directed the manuscript volumes
of his lectures to be burned in his lifetime, and the
following letter, written by him to Hume, in April, 1773,
apparently in contemplation of a journey to London,
shows that he had but little confidence in his own judgment as to what he had done :—

"MY DEAR FRIEND,—As I have left the care of all my
literary papers to you, I must tell you that except those
which I carry along with me, there are none worth the

publication, but a fragment of a great work which contains a history of the astronomical systems that were successively in fashion down to the time of Descartes. Whether that might not be published as a fragment of an intended juvenile work, I leave entirely to your judgment, though I begin to suspect myself there is more refinement than solidity in some parts of it. This little work you will find in a thin folio paper book in my back-room. All the other loose papers, which you will find in that desk, or within the glass folding doors of a bureau which stands in my bedroom, together with about eighteen thin paper folio books, which you will likewise find within the same glass-folding doors, I desire may be destroyed without any examination. Unless I die very suddenly, I shall take care that the papers I carry with me shall be carefully sent to you.—I am ever, my dear friend, most faithfully yours,

"ADAM SMITH."

In 1787 Smith was elected Lord Rector of the University of Glasgow. "No preferment," he writes, "could have given me so much real satisfaction. No man can owe greater obligations to a society than I do to the University of Glasgow. They educated me: they sent me to Oxford. Soon after my return to Scotland, they elected me one of their own members, and afterwards preferred me to another office, to which the abilities and virtues of the never-to-be-forgotten Dr. Hutcheson had given a superior degree of illustration. The period of thirteen years which I spent as a member of that society, I remember as by far the most useful, and therefore by far the happiest and most honourable period of my life; and now, after three and twenty years' absence, to be remembered in so very agreeable a manner by my old friends and protectors, gives me a heartfelt joy which I cannot easily express to you."

As has already been mentioned, he sustained a severe shock through his mother's death in 1784. From this date his health seems to have declined. In 1790 he was prostrated by an obstruction of the bowels, which, after inflicting on him a good deal of prolonged suffering, terminated fatally in July of that year. He thus died at the comparatively early age of sixty-seven.

On the southern slope of the Calton Hill, opening off the London Road, there is a small and quiet cemetery, in a corner of which stands a plain but stately tomb, overlooking a rocky and precipitous descent. Below it, almost within a stonethrow, and in the heart of one of the most densely populated districts of Edinburgh, lies another burying-place, its gravestones blackened with the smoke and dust of the busy city. Above, there repose the remains of David Hume. Below, and not far separated from him, lies the dust of his dearest friend.

CHAPTER III.

WE now approach the subject of this book in his capacity of a moralist. Had his ethical writings not assumed a systematic form, but been presented as a series of essays, written by an acute observer of men and things, upon the nature of certain human emotions, Adam Smith would, in all probability, have taken rank as one of the greatest essayists in English literature. The style is the simple, direct, eighteenth-century style which is the envy of those for whom it is a lost art. The writer has the acuteness and latent humour of Montaigne, while he has something of that power of subtle analysis which characterizes the highest type of latter-day novelist. But it is not in him to lay the foundations of a philosophical system. Such a system cannot, or, at all events, at the time he wrote, could not, dispense with some kind of metaphysical basis, whether that basis dogmatically ignored and excluded any metempirical existence, or professed to recognize and build upon something more or less of the sort. Of what Smith taught in that first part of his fourfold course at Glasgow, which dealt with these and the like topics, we have no authentic record; but there is abundant internal evidence that it could not have been anything either very definite, or that committed him very deeply. The hesitation which both Hume and he evidently felt about the publication of the former's "Dialogues concerning Natural Religion," proves that Smith was in no hurry to enter the lists as champion of a scepticism, which in those times was as unpopular as it is popular in certain circles to-day. Besides this, during the period when these things were most in his thoughts he was a professor in a Scottish university, a position which he certainly could not have occupied had his metaphysics been unsatisfactory. Hume failed to obtain the very position Smith had held, and we may, without violence to probabilities, conjecture that the reason why a certain Mr. Clow was, as we have already seen, appointed to the chair vacated by Smith at Glasgow, in preference to both Burke and Hume, was that neither of the latter united in himself the requisites of orthodoxy and nationality. It may be, though it is hardly probable, that Smith had no taste either for metaphysics or for controversy, but if want of courage was the cause of the form assumed by his ethical system, the opinions which were repressed have taken ample vengeance. A writer on ethics so acute could not fail to make his mark as a man of letters. A philosopher so silent about the principles on which his teaching depended, could not fail to be overlooked as a scientific thinker. In every reference, excepting that of the systematic study of the subject which it professes to expound, his "Theory of Moral Sentiments" is delightful reading. As a work on Moral Philosophy it is dull and unedifying. As such, therefore, it will receive but scant notice in these pages.

To understand Smith's position as a philosopher, properly so called, it is above all things necessary to bear in
mind his position in history.   With Locke a revival
had taken place in British philosophy.   Locke 'invented,'
(the term is more accurate than 'discovered,') and
applied to the facts of experience, a method which was
his own so far as psychology was concerned.

Bacon had called men back to the investigation of the
facts of experience as the foundation of knowledge.
His method was what is popularly called inductive.   It
proceeded from particular instances to general par-
ticulars, and like all scientific methods it really got along
by first inventing hypotheses and testing their truth afterwards.   The success of such a method is, of course,
dependent as much upon the scope of the imagination
of the observer in framing hypotheses, as on the accuracy
of the verification.

By pursuing this method, Locke put together a body
of psychological knowledge which rested on a metaphysical basis.   Most of his psychology was, and still is, of
the greatest value.   But the metaphysical assumptions,
the worst features of which were the doctrines of what in
the Scottish philosophy was afterwards known as Repre-
sentative Perception, and of a supposed abstract idea of
Substance, were highly vulnerable.   All our knowledge,
according to Locke, consists in "the view the mind has
of its own ideas."   "A quality in an object is the power
to produce any idea in my mind."   The mind was for
him a *tabula rasa*, upon which 'substance' imprinted
ideas.   "Not imagining how these simple ideas can
subsist of themselves, **we** accustomed ourselves to

suppose some substratum wherein they do subsist, and from which they do result; which, therefore, we call substance."

Bishop Berkeley made short work of the theory of Substance. He put the "New Question," what does Substance mean for those who hold that all knowledge has its origin in sense perception? His answer was that Locke's 'substance' was a meaningless attempt at an abstract, and therefore impossible, idea. There could be but one true conception of the objective world, the conception of it as a series of sensations and groups of sensations impressed upon the human mind by the only existence which, according to Berkeley, was at once independent of it, and intelligible, the Supreme Being. Hume accepted the criticism of Locke's theory of Substance put forward by Berkeley, and proceeded to make havoc of the edifice which the latter had reared in its place. What intelligible meaning had either the mental substance upon which Berkeley imagined sensations to be impressed, or the Deity who so impressed them, for those who, like Berkeley and himself, thought that all knowledge had its source in sensation? None at all! Custom and the laws of association were responsible for the fiction that we ourselves had any existence apart from our momentary experiences, or that these experiences had any cause or validity otherwise than as our ideas. It was this conclusion which Kant critically examined, with the result that in his view Hume's reasoning proved too much, if carried to its logical conclusions, and made even the presupposed fact of a sequence of sensations an impossibility. He went back to Hume's premises, the principles of Locke, and, agreeing that in point of *time*, sensation and not thought was the *prius* in the individual, proceeded to show that the individual experience in which sensation became a fact, and the space and time which were the forms of that experience, themselves implied, as their logical *prius*, an intelligence *for* which alone they could exist. With Kant and his successors we have nothing to do here. What concerns us is to state the position of philosophy in the hands of David Hume, who obviously had a deep influence in this reference upon his friend Smith. In morals, Hume was not, in the ordinary sense, a utilitarian. His method was to take what he conceived to be the facts, and apply to them the Baconian method. His philosophical standpoint of course led him to endeavour to resolve the facts of our moral experience into the simplest elements possible. A man for whom self meant only a series of really unrelated sensations, was not likely to set up, as the object of conduct, the attainment of ends dependent on a complicated conception of a self which for him was more or less of a metaphysical figment. He took the good and bad tendencies in human nature as he found them, and dealt with them by the same method as he had already applied to the analysis of the relations of cause and effect. His method was likewise the method of Adam Smith, and the metaphysical and psychological presuppositions on which it was made to depend, in the case of Hume explicitly, were those on which the " Theory of Moral Sentiments " was dependent implicitly.

Hume's application of the experimental method to the investigation of the phenomena of moral life had made it plain to him that the chief feature in these phenomena was the approval of the qualities which are recognized as meritorious. The facts of the case were inconsistent with a reference of this approval to self-love as its origin. Seeking this origin elsewhere, he adopted a view of it which rested on a disinterested benevolence, apparently independent of any merely self-regarding point of view: " The hypothesis which we countenance is plain. It maintains that morality is determined by sentiment. It defines virtue to be whatever mental action or quality gives to a spectator the pleasing sentiment of approbation, and vice the contrary." [1]

This statement by Hume of his theory puts us in a position to form a just estimate of the nature of the contribution of Adam Smith to the elucidation of the problem of the nature of moral qualities. The 'sentiment,' which for Hume was the great fact, demanded a close investigation, and to such an investigation Smith subjected it. With Hume moral sentiment was closely connected with some kind of perception of the useful consequences, (useful not merely to the individual but to the race,) of moral conduct. With Smith a moral judgment is really an expression of the sympathy of an impartial spectator with the impulses which occasion action. Take, for example, conscience. " We either approve," he says, " or disapprove of the conduct of another man according as we feel that, when we bring his case home to ourselves, we either can or cannot entirely sympathize with the

[1] Appendix I. to " Essay concerning the Principles of Morals."

sentiments and motives which directed it. And, in the same manner, we either approve or disapprove of our own conduct according as we feel that, when we place ourselves in the situation of another man, and view it, as it were, with his eyes and from his station, we either can or cannot entirely enter into and sympathize with the sentiments and motives which influenced it. We can never survey our own sentiments and motives, we can never form any judgment regarding them, unless we remove ourselves, as it were, from our own natural station, and endeavour to view them as at a certain distance from us." Like all persons who proceed inductively, Smith applied his preconceived hypothesis to the facts, and tested its accordance with them. His hypothesis was that the phenomena which had attracted the attention of Hume, as well as of Shaftesbury and Hutcheson, might be explained as the result of a natural instinct of sympathy or fellow-feeling. His ethical writings consist of illustrations of the application of his hypothesis.

" The Theory of Moral Sentiments " opens with a description of sympathy as a principle of human nature which interests man in the fortune of others, and renders their happiness necessary to him, although he derives nothing from it except the pleasure of seeing it. The emotion in question denotes, speaking generally, our fellow feeling with any passion whatever. Applying this explanation to what is commonly recognized as the propriety or impropriety of actions, the just result arrived at may be summarized thus : When the original passions of the person principally concerned are in perfect concord with the sympathetic emotions of the spectator, they necessarily appear to him just and proper; and when, on the contrary, he finds that they do not coincide with what he feels, they necessarily appear to him unjust and improper, and unsuitable to the causes which excite them. To approve of the passions of another as suitable to their objects, is the same thing as to observe that we entirely sympathize with them; and not to approve of them as such, is the same thing as to observe that we do not entirely sympathize with them. The character of the book, and its style, are far more those of a volume of literary essays, devoted to the purpose of expanding these propositions, than what one naturally expects in a philosophical treatise. The method of Hume is there, but we lack his precision, and that grasp of the whole which is never wanting in his pages. The truth is that Smith was never quite in his place as a professor of Moral Philosophy. He was essentially an observer of the external world of men and things. When he takes to introspection, his analyses are those of the essayist rather than of the psychologist. But from the point of view of literature they are admirable, for they possess the supreme quality of truthfulness. Take, for example, the following remarks upon what he speaks of as the passions which take their origin from the body :—

"It is indecent to express any strong degree of those passions which arise from a certain situation or disposition of the body; because the company, not being in the same disposition, cannot be expected to sympathize with them. Violent hunger, for example, though upon many occasions not only natural but unavoidable, is always indecent; and to eat voraciously is universally regarded as a piece of ill manners. There is, however, some degree of sympathy even with hunger. It is agreeable to see our companions eat with a good appetite, and all expressions of loathing are offensive. . . .

"It is quite otherwise with those passions which take their origin from the imagination. The frame of my body can be but little affected by the alterations which are brought about on that of my companions; but my imagination is more ductile, and more readily assumes, if I may say so, the shape and configuration of the imaginations of those with whom I am familiar. A disappointment in love, or ambition, will, upon this account, call forth more sympathy than the greatest bodily evil. Those passions arise altogether from the imagination.

"The person who has lost his whole fortune, if he is in health, feels nothing in his body. What he suffers is from the imagination only, which represents to him the loss of his dignity, neglect from his friends, contempt from his enemies—dependence, want, and misery coming fast upon him; and we sympathize with him the more strongly upon this account, because our imaginations can the more readily mould themselves upon his imagination than our bodies can mould themselves upon his body. The loss of a leg may generally be regarded as a more real calamity than the loss of a mistress. It would be a ridiculous tragedy, however, of which the catastrophe was to turn upon a loss of this kind. A misfortune of the other kind, how frivolous soever it may appear to be, has given occasion to many a fine one."

This is fine writing. Its matter and manner are as good as those of Montaigne, and there is a purpose super-added. Subtle analysis of this kind is never so pleasing as when it comes before us incidentally, as it were, and in the form of a means to an end. It is wonderful that the "Theory of Moral Sentiments" has not become more popular as general reading. In a literary reference it is a far greater book than it ever can be in the con-templation of the mere student of the history of philo-sophy. The passage quoted reminds one of Schopenhauer. when he is at his best. It goes to the very root of the whole matter in its subtle apprehension of the most delicate of distinctions.

We are now in a position to describe, in its outline, Smith's ethical system. The guide to it is throughout the theory of sympathy stated above. It has already been suggested that the foundation of "The Theory of Moral Sentiments" was not of a Utilitarian character. Hume was far too keen and sceptical an observer to put forward a theory so difficult to reconcile with the facts of experience as one which should find the guiding principle of conduct in the tendency to seek self. And Adam Smith was equally cautious. He looked to the facts, and among the facts he found unselfishness staring him in the face. Take the opening sentences of his book: " How selfish soever man may be supposed, there are evidently some principles in his nature which interest him in the fortune of others, and render their happiness necessary to him, though he derives nothing from it except the pleasure of seeing it. Of this kind is pity or compas-sion, the emotion which we feel for the misery of others, when we either see it or are made to conceive it, in a very lively manner.'

Hume, his somewhat cynical scepticism again predominating, had thrown out the suggestion that our sympathetic pleasure and displeasure at the moral or immoral conduct of others, was due to our perception of the tendencies of the respective actions, and their probable effects on the well-being of the race. Not so Smith. He is fonder of, and more true to, facts than was even Hume. (He finds that the essential element in moral sentiment is a direct sympathy with the motives, and not with the consequences, of action. Upon this point he is quite clear. Nor does he seek to go behind the facts, or to find any explanation for them. He is content to treat this phenomenon of sympathy as original and irresoluble. It is not easy to find in the "Theory" any reason for the plan he adopts in the investigations he bases on his discovery. First of all, he proceeds to explain our sense of the propriety of actions. This, he declares, depends upon the extent to which the motive or feeling of the person principally concerned accords with the feeling of the spectator. "The man whose sympathy keeps time to my grief, cannot but admit the reasonableness of my sorrow. He who laughs at the same joke, and laughs along with me, cannot well deny the propriety of my laughter. On the contrary, the person who upon these different occasions, either feels no such emotion as I feel, or feels more than bears any proportion to mine, cannot avoid disapproving my sentiments on account of their dissonance with his own." There are two kinds of sympathy, an agreeable and a disagreeable kind. And

Smith will not admit that there is any inconsistency in the admission into his system of a disagreeable sympathy, arising from the general proposition which he lays down that the sentiment of approbation, which is always agreeable, is founded on sympathy. For, as he points out, in the sentiment of approbation there are two things to be taken notice of; first, the sympathetic passion of the spectator; and secondly, the emotion which arises from his observing the perfect coincidence between this sympathetic passion in himself, and the original passion in the person principally concerned. It is this last emotion, according to Smith, in which the sentiment of approbation properly consists, an emotion which is always agreeable and delightful. The other may be either agreeable or disagreeable, according to the nature of the original passion, whose features it must always in some measure retain. In the chapters which deal with this subject there are some fine specimens of analysis. That which discusses the effect upon individuals of a weaker calibre of the manifestations of a coarse, strong nature, is especially worth remembering. " The hoarse, boisterous, and discordant voice of anger, when heard at a distance, inspires us with fear or aversion. We do not fly towards it, as to one who cries out with pain and agony. Women and men of weak nerves tremble and are overcome with fear, though sensible that themselves are not the objects of the anger. They conceive fear, however, by putting themselves in the situation of the person who is so. Even those of stouter hearts are disturbed; not indeed enough to make them afraid, but enough to make them angry; for anger is the passion which they would feel in

the situation of the other person. It is the same **case**
with hatred. Mere expressions of spite inspire it against
nobody but the man who uses them. Both these passions
are by nature the objects of our aversion. Their disagreeable and boisterous appearance never excites, never
prepares, and often disturbs our sympathy. Grief does
not more powerfully engage and attract us to the person
in whom we observe it, than these, while we are ignorant
of their cause, disgust and detach us from him. It was,
it seems, the intention of nature that these rougher
and more unamiable emotions, which drive men from
one another, should be less easily and more rarely com-
municated."

The next topic to which the theory of sympathy is
applied is that of merit and demerit, or the objects of
reward and punishment. We do not thoroughly and
heartily sympathize with the gratitude of one man towards
another, merely because that other has been the cause of
his good fortune. But when to the beneficent tendency
of an action is joined the propriety of the affection from
which it proceeds, then Smith holds that the action is a
meritorious one. It is, in short, the propriety or impropriety of the motive, from the point of view of a
spectator capable of sympathy, which determines the
moral quality of the action.

The weakness of all this as a theory of morals is
apparent. Everything turns upon the subjective condition
of a supposed spectator. But every spectator is an
individual. Therefore Smith makes the nature and
validity of ethical principles depend on the state of
mind of an individual. He seeks to lessen this difficulty

by supposing the spectator to be an impartial one, but it is needless to remark that this supposition does not avail for escape from the difficulty. The dilemma is exhaustive. Every system of morals must either be hedonistic (that is, based upon the pleasurable impulses of the particular individual), or else depend on some principle to which validity is ascribed apart from the particular experiences of the person who forms a moral judgment based on it. It is just because Smith does not face this dilemma, and accept one or other of the alternatives, that his system has become of little or no account as a contribution to philosophy.

The third important subject dealt with in the book, is the foundation of our judgments concerning our own sentiments and conduct, and of the sense of duty. This embraces the theory of conscience. Man desires, according to Adam Smith, not only to be loved, but to be lovely. The love and admiration which we naturally conceive for those whose character and conduct we approve of, necessarily dispose us to desire to become ourselves the objects of the like agreeable sentiments, and to be as amiable and as admirable as those whom we admire the most. The most sincere praise can give but little pleasure when it cannot be considered as some sort of proof of praiseworthiness. Nature has endowed us, not only with a desire of being approved of, but with a desire of being what ought to be approved of, or of being what we ourselves approve in other men. This explains how it is that profligate criminals have frequently but little sense of the baseness of their own conduct, and regard with comparative equanimity death upon the gibbet as a mere piece of bad luck which has befallen them. Such men conquer the fear of death easily because of this. The innocent man, on the other hand, over and above the uneasiness which the nature of death may cause him, is tormented by his own indignation at the injustice which has been done him, when he is wrongly condemned. Pain, as Smith is never tired of reminding us, is, in almost all cases, a more pungent sensation than the opposite and correspondent pleasure. The one depresses us much more below the natural state of our happiness than the other raises us above it. Hence the wise man will often feel severely the injustice of unmerited censure, while he will reject with contempt unmerited applause. Such is the origin and nature of conscience. Some of the most profound and weighty observations in all the writings of the author of the theory are to be found in the chapters which deal with it.

The remaining great topic of the "Theory of Moral Sentiments" is the character of virtue. The man who acts according to the rules of perfect prudence, of strict justice, and of proper benevolence, may be said to be perfectly virtuous, although the most perfect knowledge of the rules of conduct, if it is not supported by the most perfect self-command, will not always enable him to do his duty. These propositions initiate an investigation too detailed to be sketched in these pages, even in outline, but well worth a careful perusal. Smith is never so good as when he is writing in the strain adopted here. There is no affectation, no insincerity about him. Nor has he anything of the prude in his composition. He was a wise, just man, or at least one who knew well what wisdom and justice meant. And his style in treating of these things is excellent. He is never heavy, even when he is as diffuse as often happens with him. It has already been remarked that had he devoted his powers as a moralist to essay writing, instead of to the composition of a systematic treatise, he might have attained high distinction among British men of letters. But it was not to be so, and the blame lies with the author if the public have persistently declined to look for one kind of merit in regions where the only promise held out to them is that of something quite different.

It will be convenient to take this opportunity of adverting to the literary productions of the author of the "Theory of Moral Sentiments," other than the "Wealth of Nations." Besides these two works, there are extant several essays of considerable length written by Smith at various periods in his career. One of these, the "Considerations concerning the First Formation of Languages," while of no general interest, exhibits the subtlety of Smith's imagination in its illustrations of the proposition that language becomes more simple in its rudiments and principles, just in proportion as it grows more complex in its composition. The author likens the gradual improvement of language to the gradual improvement of machinery, in that, instead of a particular principle being applied for the production of each single movement, a single principle is in an increasing degree so applied as to produce more than one movement. But he lays stress on the qualification of the analogy by the circumstance that, in the case of languages, the simplifications, instead of rendering the means more perfect for the fulfilment of its end, really renders it less perfect.

The essay on the "Principles which lead and direct Philosophical Enquiries as illustrated by the History of Astronomy," was left by its author in an incomplete condition. What is finished of it relates mainly to method, and to the tendencies of the mind in observation. The essays on the "Principles which lead and direct Philosophical Enquiries, illustrated by the History of the Ancient Physics," and by the "History of the Ancient Logic and Metaphysics" respectively, are of little general interest. The first mentioned of these three essays is divided into four chapters; the first dealing with the "Effects of Unexpectedness or Surprise"; the second investigating "Wonder, or the Effects of Novelty"; the third relating to the "Origin of Philosophy"; and the fourth treating of the "History of Astronomy."

There is also an essay on the "Nature of that Imitation which takes place in what are called the Imitative Arts." There is much matter here of a kind which recalls the style of the "Theory of Moral Sentiments." But as a whole, the essay is decidedly below the level of Smith's general writing. There is a characteristic comment by the bosom friend of Hume upon Hume's most aggressive enemy (Rousseau): "'Painting,' *says an author more capable of feeling strongly than of analysing accurately*, ' Painting, which presents its imitations not to the imagination, but to the senses, can represent nothing besides the objects of sight.'" Smith goes on to contrast music with painting, and both music and painting with dancing and poetry.

The brief treatise on the external senses is of no philosophical value. When Adam Smith says in it that the four qualities, or attributes, of extension, divisibility, figure, and mobility, or the capacity of motion or rest, seem necessarily involved in the idea or conception of a solid substance, one feels instinctively that he had never taken kindly either to his Berkeley or to his Hume. There is in this essay, among other things, a repetition of the even then somewhat hackneyed psychological tale of Cheselden's observations upon the growth of vision in the young gentleman whom he couched for cataract.

The only other production by Smith which remains to us, is a brief fragment upon the affinity between certain English and Italian Verses. What was in the mind of the author of the treatises, some complete, and some fragmentary upon all these subjects, is not difficult to divine. He probably contemplated a series of great works upon the various phases of intellectual life which were embraced in his course of lectures at Glasgow University. What he completed embraced the theories of Ethics and of Political Economy. What he failed to complete would have covered the field of those general subjects which lay between these theories, including a systematic view of the science of Jurisprudence.

CHAPTER IV.

ON February 17, 1792, two years after Adam Smith's death, a famous debate took place in the House of Commons. The Commons having resolved themselves into a committee of the whole House, the Earl of Morn ington in the chair, to consider so much of his Majesty's speech in the opening of the Session as related to the public income and expenditure, Mr. Pitt rose and addressed the committee. After explaining the several measures which he proposed to introduce for the relief of the British taxpayer, he proceeded to discuss the causes of the rapid increase which at that time was taking place in the manufacturing industries of the country. Among these he placed one which may best be described in his own words :—

"But there is still another cause, even more satisfactory than these, because it is of a still more extensive and permanent nature; that constant accumulation of capital, that continual tendency to increase, the operation of which is universally seen in a greater or less proportion, whenever it is not obstructed by some public calamity, or by some mistaken or mischievous policy, but which must be conspicuous and rapid indeed in any country which has once arrived at an advanced state of commercial prosperity. Simple and obvious as this principle is, and felt and observed as it must have been in a greater or less degree, even from the earliest periods, I doubt whether it has ever been fully developed and sufficiently explained, but in the writings of an author of our times, now, unfortunately, no more (I mean the author of a celebrated treatise on the wealth of nations), whose extensive knowledge of detail and philosophical research will, I believe, furnish the best solution to every question connected with the history of commerce or with the systems of political economy."

No words express better than this language of Pitt the completeness of the recognition of the change which Adam Smith had effected in public opinion by his new view of the problem which he set himself to investigate. That problem was not abstract, but concrete. The question was the great one of the nature of the production and accumulation of wealth in a community containing men and institutions of a certain and definite kind—just such a kind as would rise up in image before the minds of an assemblage of the Commons of England, sitting in the later part of the eighteenth century. One of the secrets of the great popularity of "The Wealth of Nations" was this concrete quality. Its author united in himself two powers which do not often go together, the power of abstract thinking, and that of being able to grasp facts with a keen interest in them merely as facts This it is

which has made his book immortal in its influence on
statesmen of all ways of thinking. We know that on
Pitt it exercised a profound influence from the first time
he read it, and he read it often.   On three great
occasions it completely determined his policy.   The first
was that on which he laid down his financial principles in
the speech just quoted; the second was his refusal to
support a Bill brought in in 1795 by Mr. Samuel Whit-
bread, the then member for Bedford, to regulate the
wages of labourers in husbandry; and the third was his
resolute insistence that the Government should, in 1800,
abstain from interference in the purchase of corn in
foreign markets, on the ground that the speculations of
private individuals afforded the greatest prospect of producing a sufficient supply.

Whether or not Adam Smith is correctly represented as having maintained in theory that political
economy is a body of abstract and immutable principles, he certainly did not himself lay down any such
principles.   On the contrary, he was describing the
Great Britain of his time, of the time of Pitt and
Fox, the Britain which was, within less than a century
from the period at which he wrote, to realize to the
full his conception of what it might become, were
the practical changes which he advocated carried into
effect.   It has been said by Mr. Bagehot that he prepared
the way for, though he did not found, the abstract science
of Political Economy.   No doubt this is in a sense true.
Adam Smith was not, like Ricardo, a man who started
from certain propositions and deduced a system from
them.   But it is this absence of system that has been his

very merit, and that has made him, with all his faults, probably the greatest economist that ever lived. He had a perception that abstract propositions, however carefully stated, express only one aspect or side of things, and are therefore wanting in truth, a quality which belongs to what is concrete alone. Abstractions are useful servants, but bad masters. Seeing this, he is always looking to the one side or the other, and digressing, often tediously, but never unprofitably, into discussions of those real details of commerce and politics which are so rarely subjected to any scientific treatment. This is why it is that his book is diffuse and lacking in arrangement. But its very vices give it a meaning and an interest to men who would otherwise have neither the opportunity nor the capacity to profit by it.

Before attempting to give some account of what Smith taught the world of his time, in "The Wealth of Nations," it is desirable to state shortly what it was that that world thought before it had digested his book, and what was the nature and origin of the prejudices which the new teacher once for all broke down. Of these thoughts and prejudices the best known and most important were what have become familiar in history as the mercantile and agricultural systems.

It is a common kind of mistake to exaggerate, and give an undue prominence to, a fallacy which has been exposed and laid. Nothing is more usual in ordinary conversation than to hear that the mistake, which an unsuccessful opponent of the person speaking has made, was something so transparent that those who are not familiar with the misleading character of adverse representations of other people's positions, wonder how **any** human being of ordinary intelligence could have committed such a fallacy. But the reasoning of the world, or at all events that which is best in it, is not carried on in syllogistic form. It is always elliptical, and sometimes not even merely that. Real, as distinguished from notional, assent is not generally to be obtained by the application of the rules of logic. Consequently there is great room everywhere for error, even of a purely formal character. We see only one side of a subject at a time, and often not even so much. The advocates of the mercantile system did not in terms make wealth and money identical, as they are crudely represented to have done. If they had, they would quickly have been found out and exposed. But it is none the less accurate to say that this was the tendency of their reasonings, and the common element in the mistakes they committed, notwithstanding that they did not know it to be so. How natural it was that this should be the case, the merest glance at the history of the doctrine will show.

The mercantile system arose out of the decomposition of feudalism and mediævalism. The days had gone by in which war was the only important subject in Western civilization; commerce was becoming more and more important. The merchant and the landowner found it to their advantage to pay for the soldiers who composed the standing armies under the new order of things, instead of themselves taking a constant part in supplying the materials out of which these armies were composed. A great development of industry ensued, a development the accomplishment of which depended for its success upon the possession of the requisite capital. The discoveries of the art of printing; of the routes over the sea to the East and to America; of improvements in the machinery of production—all contributed to make the possession by a nation of wealth more than equivalent to the mere possession of that bone and muscle which could be hired from abroad for money.

It was natural that the gold and silver, which in every civilized country was appreciated as symbolical of the possession of power of this kind, should come to be identified in the popular imagination with wealth itself. Wealth was then, as now, an abstract term. The products of labour had their value best measured in money, and the measure, which was concrete and easily conceived, was readily identified in the popular imagination with the wealth which it measured, particularly when one of the prominent uses which that wealth served was to command the services of paid soldiers and sailors. The object then of a nation being admittedly to grow rich, and riches meaning the accumulation within its territories of the precious metals, it was natural that mercantile and legislative policy should be shaped accordingly. Now when we sell goods we receive money; when we buy them we pay it out. Therefore let us sell to foreign customers as much as we can, and buy not at all. So reasoned the predecessors of Adam Smith. The multitude, however able the particular individuals scattered here and there among it, is prone to follow custom in its reasoning. Even where that multitude is relatively small, and its component units relatively intelligent, this proposition holds good, though in a less degree. A litigant

who employs half a dozen competent counsel to conduct
his case where two would be sufficient, sometimes finds
that his case is not only imperfectly, but also unintelli-
gently dealt with. The British House of Commons is
infinitely unintelligent on points of detail of little or no
difficulty. Men are like sheep, gregarious in their
fallacies. Thus it was that the mercantile system was
not, at an early period, formulated and exposed, as it
would have been had six men instead of several nations
been responsible for it.

It has been said that the mercantile system was
really, in practice as distinguished from theory, a set of
tendencies, commonly found in combination, though
severally prevailing in different degrees in different
minds. These tendencies have been summed up as—
the over-estimation of the importance of possessing a
large quantity of the precious metals; an improper esti-
mation of the relation of foreign to domestic trade; the
undue exaltation of the industries which work up materials over those that provide them; and an undue readi-
ness to invoke State interference for commercial purposes.
It would seem that the last two of these kinds of
tendencies are consequences of the first. How they
came to be so is well explained by Smith himself.

After pointing out that one result of the policy above
described was an attempt on the part of the different
nations of Europe to prohibit the exportation of the
precious metals, he goes on to show that as these
countries became more engrossed with commerce, their
merchants found the restriction extremely inconvenient.
They could often most conveniently buy goods for im-

portation in foreign markets by paying for these goods in gold and silver. They came, therefore, to represent, first, that the exportation of gold and silver, in order to purchase foreign goods, did not always diminish the quantity of those metals in the kingdom. That, on the contrary, it might frequently increase the quantity, because, if the consumption of foreign goods was not thereby increased, those goods might be re-exported to foreign countries, and being there sold for a large profit, might bring back much more treasure than was originally sent to purchase them. They represented, secondly, that the prohibition could not hinder the exportation of gold and silver, which, on account of the smallness of their bulk in proportion to their value, could easily be smuggled abroad. That this exportation could only be prevented by a proper attention to what they called the balance of trade. That when the country exported to a greater value than it imported, a balance became due to it from foreign nations, which was necessarily paid to it in gold and silver, and thereby increased the quantity of those metals in the kingdom. But that when it imported to a greater value than it exported, a contrary balance became due to foreign nations, which was necessarily paid to them in the same manner, and thereby diminished that quantity. That in this case to prohibit the exportation of these metals could not prevent it, but only by making it more dangerous render it more expensive. That the exchange was merely turned more against the country which owed the balance than it otherwise might have been; the merchant who purchased a bill upon the foreign country being obliged to

6

pay the banker who sold it, not only for the natural risk, trouble, and expense of sending the money thither, but for the extraordinary risk arising from the prohibition. But that the more the exchange was against any country, the more the balance of trade became necessarily against it, the money of that country becoming necessarily of so much less value in comparison with that of the country to which the balance was due.

Smith pointed out that arguments of this kind were partly solid and partly sophistical. They were solid so far as they asserted that the exportation of gold and silver in trade might frequently be advantageous to the country. They were solid, too, in asserting that no prohibition could prevent their exportation when private people found any advantage in it. But they were sophistical in supposing that either to preserve or to augment the quantity of those metals required more the attention of Government than to preserve or to augment the quantity of any other useful commodity, which the freedom of trade, without any such attention, never fails to supply in the proper quantity. They were sophistical, perhaps, also, in asserting that the high price of exchange necessarily increased what they called the unfavourable balance of trade, or occasioned the exportation of a greater quantity of gold and silver. That high price, indeed, was extremely disadvantageous to the merchants who had any money to pay in foreign countries. They paid so much dearer for the bills which their bankers granted them upon these countries. But though the risk arising from the prohibition might occasion some extraordinary expense to the bankers, it would not necessarily carry any more money out of the country. This expense would generally be laid out in the country in smuggling the money out of it, and could seldom occasion the exportation of a single sixpence beyond the sum drawn for. The high price of exchange, too, would naturally dispose the merchants to endeavour to make their exports balance their imports, in order that they might have this high exchange to pay upon as small a sum as possible. The high price of exchange, besides, must necessarily have operated as a tax in raising the price of foreign goods, and thereby diminished their consumption. It would tend, therefore, not to increase, but to diminish what they called the unfavourable balance of trade, and consequently the exportation of gold and silver.

But the arguments of the merchants, insufficient though they were, prevailed with those to whom they were addressed in exactly the way intended. The most famous of these converts, the one to whom Adam Smith does not tire of alluding, was Colbert, the great minister of Louis XIV. Colbert was by no means a bigoted adherent of the mercantile system. He saw its weakness, but he was none the less strongly attached to it as a means of developing the resources of France. The industry and commerce of that country he proceeded to regulate much as he would have regulated the departments of a public office. The State interfered at every turn. Not only did he confer privileges on some industries, and impose disabilities on others, but he favoured the industries of the towns at the expense of the industries of the country. In order to encourage the manufactures of the great cities by rendering provisions cheap, he prohibited the exportation of corn altogether, to the great disadvantage of the farmers of France. But if the benefit was outweighed by the cost of securing it, if the public were taxed for the sake of particular enterprizes, at least the manufactures of France flourished under Colbert. It is a fault which all free-traders are prone to commit (and Adam Smith was hardly more free from it than his successors have been), that they overstate their case. If the aim be, as all the old and most of the new economists have assumed it to be, to increase to a maximum the aggregate production of wealth in a particular community, unquestionably free-dom in trade is the best means to adopt for its accomplish-ment. But in the process, particular industries, such as the sugar-refining industry in our times, may and do suffer. This fact affords no argument against free-trade, but its denial affords an opening for the attack of an enemy, who otherwise would have none. Colbert was no blind protectionist. He saw what he was about. He developed the commerce of France much as Prince Bismarck has developed that of Germany. And it is as much, and no more, a moot point to-day whether France did not get value for the price she paid in the seventeenth century under Colbert, as it is a moot point whether Germany has not benefited on balance by the policy of Bismarck. The fallacy of the protectionist lies in the suggestion that it is equally a moot point whether the system of these statesmen would be beneficial if applied to a country the commerce of which has become, as is the case of the United Kingdom and the United States, fully developed.

What was going on in France in the end of the seventeenth and beginning of the eighteenth centuries was also
going on in England.   In both countries the State was
interfering, to an extent which was irritating to the
apostles of freedom, with the affairs of individuals.   The
result was a reactionary movement, which, like all reactionary movements, whether Conservative or Liberal in their
tendencies, was presently carried to an extreme.   Mercantileism had become associated with the power, not merely
of Governments, but of those aristocracies which at that
time represented Governments.   It was in France that
the movement against this state of things, both in politics
and in political economy, took most definite shape.   The
doctrines of Rousseau and of Voltaire had their counterpart in the tendencies of the time.   The Encyclopædists
of Paris became closely identified with a school of
economists who were violently and bitterly opposed to
mercantileism; a school of which it is evident that both
Hume and Smith saw much during their respective
sojourns in Paris.   Agriculture was at this time in a most
depressed condition, and it was neither unnatural nor
unreasonable that the cause of this condition should be
sought in the restrictions which the State had imposed
on the free pursuit of agricultural industry.   But the
complaint did not stop here.   Men found out, or thought
they had found out, that agriculture was the only pursuit
which was really productive.   Agriculture does, they
maintained, really add to the quantity of materials
available for the purposes of man.   How different it is
with the so-called manufacturing industries !   The labour
of the artificer replaces only the stock which employs

him, together with its ordinary profits. The stock consists in the materials, tools, and wages necessary for his employment and maintenance, and advanced to him by his employer. Its profits are the fund destined for the maintenance of the employer himself. The profits of manufacturing stock are not, therefore, like the rent of land, a net produce, which remains after completely paying the whole expense which must be laid out in order to obtain them. The stock of the farmer yields him a profit as well as that of the master-manufacturer, and it yields a rent likewise to another person, which that of the master-manufacturer does not. The expense, therefore, laid out in employing and maintaining workmen and manufacturers does no more than continue the existence of its own value, and does not produce any new value. It is therefore altogether a barren and unproductive expense. The expense, on the other hand, laid out in employing farmers and country labourers, over and above continuing the existence of its own value, produces a new value, the rent of the land. It is therefore a productive expense.

We have given these statements of the mercantile and agricultural systems as nearly as possible in Adam Smith's words, because it is important to realize accurately the point of view from which he challenged them. He never was a bigoted adherent of abstract principles. He took things as he found them. He saw that the former system was exercising an evil influence on the ideas of the British Government of the time in relation to trade and commerce generally.

From the point of view of expediency he criticized these ideas. The agriculturalists were in a different position. In this country their doctrines had made little or no way. Smith's duty was merely to separate the elements of truth from the fallacies which were to be found in their teachings, and to warn the public against the latter. But while he gave this warning, he was none the less deeply indebted to the teaching of the school. Its doctrines could not fail to be fascinating to any man who knew, and appreciated, the purity of the motives of two of their chief exponents, Quesnay and Turgot. Quesnay was one of those eminent Frenchmen with whom Smith had become intimate when in France. He speaks of him as one whose system of political economy, "with all its imperfections," was "the nearest approximation to the truth that has yet been published on the principles of that very important science." And his admiration for Quesnay as a man was not less. We know that it was only his death that prevented Smith from dedicating to him "The Wealth of Nations." Of Turgot it is not necessary to speak here. The record of his life, and of his noble failure to save France, is one of those few records which seem to exercise an increasing influence upon us as time interposes an evergrowing barrier between our generation and that in which its hero lived. Turgot and Quesnay were both associated with that new school of thinkers whose work it was to burst the bonds by which France was held down in their time. If the theory of natural rights and of a social contract, the consequent equality of all men, and the limited nature of the title of the State to interfere, is not the be-all and end-all of human thought, at least it is a theory to which we, who live in the latter part of the nineteenth century, owe too much not to regard it with affectionate reverence. No false fear of the consequences of following out their premises to their conclusions prevented our forefathers from working out for us the political salvation which they failed to attain for themselves.

We have seen the general nature of the two great fallacies with which Adam Smith had to grapple, and it only remains, before proceeding to the story of how he did so, to glance very briefly at the literature of political economy at the time when he wrote.

Whatever may be the case in literature, strictly so-called, it has rarely, if ever, happened in science and philosophy that the originality of the world's men of genius has displayed itself in a great deal more than the form in which they have stated what they had to say. When we understand the exact nature of the previously existing doctrine at any particular period in the history of either of these two great departments of intellectual activity, it is easy to throw the step taken in the next period into the shape of an inference from what went before. The more, for example, mathematicians attend to the investigations of Pascal into the theory of indivisibles; of Descartes, Fermat, and Barrow into the application of algebra to geometry, and the development in their hands of the infinitesimal method, the less astonishing does the apparent creation of the infinitesimal calculus in the hands of Newton and Leibnitz appear. Again, the Platonic theory of Ideas comes in the light of a mere logical necessity to any one who has grasped the doctrine that all things, including the material elements in sense-perception, are in the state of flux asserted by Heraclitus of Ephesus. For this proposition we have the authority of Plato himself in the " Theaetetus," and we need not resort to the more doubtful authority of Lassalle. In precisely the same sense there was much to suggest to the intellect of a Darwin the theories of Natural Selection and of the Origin of Species.

If in pure literature the case is different, the reason is not far to seek. In literature, and especially in poetry, what may be called form predominates. In poetry there is much that can only be conveyed in verse. Poetry, as Goethe used to say, is form, and form is essentially the product of the individuality of its author. Therefore it is that literature never gets out of date ; that men can read Homer and Horace to-day with as little sense of the interval between their time and ours as they can read Milton and Shakespeare. Whereas, if we try to extract knowledge from Galen, or from the writings of the Bologna Aristotelians, we shall find ourselves out of sympathy with their ideas, from the absence on their part of relationship to what we regard as the context of knowledge. There are, of course, apparent exceptions. There is absolutely nothing in the writings of his German and English predecessors which throws light on the invention by Kant of the hypothesis that intelligence constitutes experience, and not experience intelligence. But in such a case we see that his exception is apparent only, when we reflect that the consequence of pushing the inferences which Hume drew from Bishop Berkeley's premises only a very little further than Hume himself pushed them, is apparently to suggest, as a necessity of the situation, the very theory which Kant devised. Kant, in fact, stands to Hume much in the same relation as Plato does to Heraclitus.

If Hume indirectly prepared the ground for Kant, he directly prepared it for Adam Smith. The intellectual life of Smith can, in truth, no more than his social life, be separated from that of Hume. Take, for example, Hume's essay on "The Balance of Trade." Sir William Petty, Sir Dudley North, and Locke had already exposed the unsoundness of the mercantile system. Hume therefore writes about it with a confidence which is the counterpart of the inimitable ease of his style. After laughing at the current apprehensions in regard to a wrong balance of trade, and declaring that they appear to be of the nature which discovers itself whenever "one is out of humour with the ministry, or is in low spirits," he formulates what he calls a 'general argument,' which is so clearly stated that it is well worth quoting :—

" Suppose four-fifths of all the money in Great Britain to be annihilated in one night, and the nation reduced to the same condition, with regard to specie, as in the reigns of the Harrys and Edwards, what would be the consequence? Must not the price of all labour and commodities sink in proportion, and everything be sold as cheap as they were in those ages? What nation could then dispute with us in any foreign market, or pretend to navigate, or to sell manufactures at the same prices which to us would afford sufficient profit? In how little time, therefore, must this bring back all the money which we had lost, and raise us to the level of all the neighbouring nations; where, after we have arrived, we immediately lose the advantage of the cheapness of labour and commodities, and the further flowing in of money is stopped by our fulness and repletion.

"Again, suppose that all the money of Great Britain were multiplied fivefold in a night, must not the contrary effect follow? Must not all labour and commodities rise to such an exorbitant height that no neighbouring nations could afford to buy from us; while their commodities, on the other hand, become so comparatively cheap that, in spite of all the laws which could be formed, they would run in upon us, and our money flow out; till we fall to a level with foreigners, and lose the great superiority of riches, which had laid us under such disadvantages?

"Now it is evident that the same causes which would correct these exorbitant inequalities, were they to happen miraculously, must prevent their happening in the ordinary course of nature, and must, for ever, in all neighbouring nations, preserve money nearly proportionable to the art and industry of each nation. All water, wherever it communicates, remains always at the same level. Ask naturalists the reason; they tell you that, were it to be raised in any one place, the superior gravity of that part not being properly balanced, must depress it, till it meets a counterpoise; and that the same cause, which redresses the inequality when it happens, must forever prevent it, without some violent internal operation."

Again, "From these principles we may learn what judgment we ought to form of those numberless bars, obstructions, and imposts, which all nations of Europe, and none more than England, have put upon trade, from an exorbitant desire of amassing money, which will never heap up beyond its level, while it circulates; or from an ill-grounded apprehension of losing their specie, which never will sink below it. Could anything scatter our riches, it would be such impolitic contrivances. But this general ill-effect, however, results from them, that they deprive neighbouring nations of that free communication and exchange which the Author of the world has intended, by giving them soils, climates, and geniuses, so different from each other. Our modern politics embrace the only method of banishing money, the using of paper credit; they reject the only method of amassing it, the practice of hoarding; and they adopt a hundred contrivances, which serve to no purpose but to check industry, and rob ourselves and our neighbours of the common benefit of art and nature."

It may probably be said, with strict accuracy, that nowhere in " The Wealth of Nations " is there a passage which refutes, with so clean a cut, or in so graceful a style, the main theory of the mercantile system. The fact is, that Smith currently gets credit for what he does not deserve, and does not get credit for what he really did. He was not the first to denounce and expose the economical heresies of the period. But he was the first to throw the true principles of modern political economy into something approaching to a systematic form, and to apply them to current political problems with a wide knowledge of the facts to which they were to be applied, as well as a complete grasp of the principles themselves.

The ideas which **we** find in the pages of Smith are many of them **to** be found in the pages of Hume's essays. But Hume had neither Smith's minute knowledge of the circumstances of the mercantile community, nor his practical instincts. That they discussed the topics of which the former treats in his essays on such subjects as Money, Interest, the Taxes, and the Public Credit, we have evidence in their correspondence. That the mind of Hume was the more original of the two we know; but it does not follow that though Hume wrote first, he could have written as he did without the suggestions and information which presumably came to him in his intercourse with his greatest and most intimate friend.

The other great writer who influenced Smith deeply, was Quesnay, of whom, as has already been remarked, he had seen a great deal during his stay in Paris. Quesnay had originally pursued the profession of medicine, in which he had attained to great eminence. Through the influence of Madame de Pompadour he had been appointed physician to Louis XV., a position where he saw much that made a deep impression on his mind. The "Maximes Générales du Gouvernement Economique," which he published by command of the king in 1758, had on it an epigraph, which is remarkable, not merely for the candour of its suggestion, but as containing the gist of the teaching of the agriculturalists or physiocrats whose chief exponent Quesnay was: " Pauvres paysans, pauvre royaume; pauvre royaume, pauvre Souverain." To regard agriculture as the only source of wealth, and from this principle to deduce a cast-iron system, was, as Smith very clearly saw, to offer an explanation of social phenomena which was wholly inadequate to the facts. The theory of government which the system necessitated by its denial of the productiveness of any industry other than agriculture, was still more clearly insufficient. The only real addition to the wealth of the community consisting, according to the school of Quesnay, in the *produit net* of the difference between the value of the sum of agricultural products and that of their cost of production, the only legitimate subject of taxation was a single impost in the nature of a land tax. But while Smith had made up his mind in common with Hume that it was altogether an error to regard manufacturing industry as unproductive, he saw very clearly that there was much light to be got from the entirely original criticisms which the political and economical consequences of the mercantile system received at the hands of Quesnay and Turgot. It is to the French writers of the physiocrat type that we must look as the other great source from which Smith derived what is characteristic in the standpoint of " The Wealth of Nations."

It became at one time a characteristic of the great writers of the English school in political economy, that they deliberately set before themselves certain abstract assumptions, and from these deduced their system. The substance of these assumptions was that men are by nature absorbed in the selfish pursuit of wealth, and that this motive is the only one we need take account of. Such was the principle which lay at the root of the system of Ricardo, and to a less degree of that of Mill. And undoubtedly political economy has gained enormously in the clearness of its doctrine by this assumption. No competent person supposed that it was strictly, or even approximately true, but they recognized in it a useful method of isolating and examining in detail the working of a certain very powerful set of tendencies in human nature. It cannot be too constantly borne in mind that political economy is not politics; that in politics we are bound to take into account the whole of the springs of action, and that so certainly as we proceed by the method of political economy, looking at one aspect only at a time, so certainly shall we come to political grief. The statutes at large contain a melancholy record of such mistakes, in the shape of Acts which, from the very fact that they over-looked motives and tendencies other than those which were in the minds of those who framed them, have either proved nugatory, or, what is worse, worked the grossest in-justice. Politics, if a science at all, is inductive and not deductive in its nature.

The method of Adam Smith is not the abstract method of the political economists who came after him. He is rather an observer, a man of the world, writing about the mercantile world in which he lived. He recognizes in the desire for wealth the most powerful of all motives, but he does not seek to exalt it into the foundation on which a system is to be based. It is just this fact that makes him somewhat unsatisfactory as a writer. He is always passing from subject to subject, after the fashion of those who observe details rather than draw conclu-sions from general features; and as the field of human nature is too wide to admit of systematic and exhaustive mapping out, we cannot avoid feeling a certain sense of dissatisfaction with his somewhat ill-arranged book. But this very defect is in another aspect a merit. Probably no one who has written before or after him has ever been so practical, or made us feel in such living contact with men and things. In Adam Smith, though he is no partizan, we see how little politics and political economy were separated in the hands of the great writers of the eighteenth century. With us, in the days when every specialist, if he is to do his work well, has to know everything that has been done in his own department, the attempt to blend the abstract investigation of human affairs with their management has certainly not proved a conspicuous success. The mixed character of Adam Smith's method is the key to his book. It prepares us for surprises of such a kind as the defence of the Navigation Acts on the ground that the national defences are more important than the accumulation of wealth, and his praise of the art of war and the advantages of a war-like spirit. He does not consider such topics irrelevant, and consequently " The Wealth of Nations " is far more a description of the industrial system of the England and Scotland of his time, and a comparison of what that system was with what it ought to have been, than a body of cosmopolitan doctrine relating to the production and distribution of wealth all over the habitable world. Bearing this fact in mind, it will be convenient, in the first place, to describe generally the character of the book, and then to go on to the statement of some of its particular teachings.

The peculiar character of the arrangement in "The Wealth of Nations," an arrangement which has caused it to be likened to a series of monographs, makes it desirable to attempt to give a brief account of the arrangement of the contents of the book. It contains four different kinds of matter: disquisitions on the science of political economy properly so-called; refutations of economical heresies which existed at its date; historical accounts of certain political institutions; and discussions on the practical application of economical principles. These four kinds of subject are kept fairly distinct in the plan of the book, and the recollection of this circumstance ought to have saved Smith from a good deal of criticism at the hands of persons who blamed his method of discussing abstract topics in close, and not always apparent, connection with those of a concrete character. The first two books are devoted to political economy proper, as the term is currently understood. The third, a short one, deals with the history of agriculture, and the rise and progress of cities and towns after the fall of the Roman Empire, and with the effect of the commerce of manufacturing towns on the agriculture of the country districts. The fourth examines and refutes the mercantile and agricultural systems; and the fifth and last is concerned with the revenue and expenditure of the commonwealth, and the principles of taxation and of State interference. We shall refer to these books in their order, making the preliminary observation that while the fourth is the one by which the author is by far the best known, the first two and the last are hardly less important. In stating his doctrine, and especially what is put forward in the first book, we shall endeavour when possible to reproduce it as nearly as practicable in the words of the original.

After declaring, not with perfect accuracy, that the annual labour of every nation is the fund that originally supplies it with all those necessaries and conveniences of life which it annually consumes, Smith commences his task with the general remark that these necessaries and conveniences consist either in the immediate produce of that labour, or in what is purchased with that produce from other nations, and further, that according as this produce, or what is purchased with it, bears a greater or less proportion to the number of those who are to consume it, the nation will be better or worse supplied. Yet this proportion must, in every nation, be regulated by two different circumstances. First, by the skill, dexterity, and judgment with which its labour is generally applied; and secondly, by the proportion between the number of those who are employed in useful labour, and of those who are not so employed. But the abundance or scantiness of this supply depends more on the former of these two circumstances than on the latter. "Among the savage nations of hunters and fishers, every individual who is able to work is more or less well employed in useful labour, and endeavours to provide, as well as he can, the necessaries and conveniences of life for himself, or such of his family or tribe as are either too old, or too young, or too infirm to go a-hunting and fishing. Such nations, however, are so miserably poor, that, from mere want, they are frequently reduced, or at least think themselves reduced, to the necessity sometimes of directly destroying, and sometimes of abandoning, their infants, their old people, and those afflicted with lingering diseases, to perish with hunger or to be devoured by wild beasts. Among civilized and thriving nations, on the contrary, though a great number of people do not labour at all, many of whom consume the produce of ten times, frequently of a hundred times more labour than the greater part of those who work; yet the produce of the whole labour of the society is so great, that all are often abundantly supplied, and a workman, even of the lowest and poorest order, if he is frugal and industrious, may enjoy a greater share of the necessaries and conveniences of life than it is possible for any savage to acquire."

Such is the passage in which Smith introduces the subject of his first book, the causes of improvement in the productive powers of labour, and the order according to which its produce is naturally distributed among the different ranks and conditions of men in society.

The first of the causes of the improvement in productive power with which he deals, he finds in the division of labour. The effects of this division he ascertains, by induction from a number of illustrations, to be three-fold: increase of dexterity in particular workmen; the saving of time, which is commonly lost in passing from one species of work to another; and the invention of machinery, which enables one man to accomplish the work of many. But how does this useful division originate? Not in prudent calculation, but in an instinct, the development of which is probably in its turn the result of reason and speech, the propensity to truck, barter, and exchange one thing for another. Only those animals which possess the faculties of reason and speech display it. " No one ever saw a dog make a fair and deliberate exchange of one bone for another, with another dog." And yet even a beggar barters the old clothes which are given to him for food or lodging. " The certainty of being able to exchange all that surplus part of the produce of his own labour, which is over and above his own consumption, for such parts of the produce of other men's labour as he may have occasion for, encourages every man to apply himself to a particular occupation, and to cultivate and bring to perfection whatever talent or genius he may possess for that particular species of business." The continuation of this passage is well worth quoting in full.

" The difference of natural talents in different men is in reality much less than we are aware of, and the very different genius which appears to distinguish men of different professions when grown up to maturity, is not, upon many occasions, so much the cause as the effect of the division of labour. The difference between the most dissimilar characters — between a philosopher and a common street porter, for example—seems to arise, not so much from nature, as from habit, custom, and education. When they came into the world, and for the first six or eight years of their existence, they were very much alike, and neither their parents nor playfellows could perceive any remarkable difference. About that age or soon after, they came to be employed in very different occupations. The difference of talents comes then to be

taken notice of, and widens by degrees, till at last the
vanity of the philosopher is willing to acknowledge scarce
any resemblance. But without the disposition to truck,
barter, and exchange, every man must have procured to
himself every necessary and conveniency of life which he
wanted. All must have had the same duties to perform
and the same work to do, and there could have been no
such difference of employment as could alone give
occasion to any great difference of talents.

"As it is this disposition which forms that difference
of talents so remarkable among men of different professions, so it is this same disposition which renders that
difference useful. Many tribes of animals, acknowledged
to be all of the same species, derive from nature a much
more remarkable distinction of genius than what, ante-
cedent to custom and education, appears to take place
among men. By nature, a philosopher is not in genius
and disposition half so different from a street porter as a
mastiff is from a greyhound, or a greyhound from a
spaniel, or this last from a shepherd's dog. These
different tribes of animals, however, though all of the
same species, are of scarce any use to one another.
The strength of the mastiff is not in the least supported
either by the swiftness of the greyhound, or by the sagacity
of the spaniel, or by the docility of the shepherd's dog.
The effects of these different geniuses and talents for
want of the power or disposition to barter and exchange,
cannot be brought into a common stock, **and** do not in
the least contribute to the better accommodation and
conveniency of the species. Each animal is still obliged
to support and defend itself separately and independently,

and derives no sort of advantage from that variety of talents with which nature has distinguished its fellows. Among men, on the contrary, the most dissimilar geniuses are of use to one another, the different produces of their respective talents by the general disposition to truck, barter, and exchange, being brought as it were into a common stock, where every man may purchase whatever part of the produce of other men's talents he has occasion for."

The next step in the argument is to show that as it is the power of exchanging that gives occasion to the division of labour, so the extent of this division must always be limited by the extent of that power, or, in other words, by the extent of the market. When the market is very small, no person can have any encouragement to dedicate himself entirely to one employment, for want of the power to exchange all that surplus produce of his own labour, which is over and above his own consumption, for such parts of the produce of other men's labours as he has occasion for. There are some sorts of industry, even of the lowest kind, which can only be carried on in a great town. A porter, for instance, can find employment and subsistence in no other place, any more than can a barrister. But for other kinds of industry, and notably for commerce, the means of transport, and especially water carriage, open up the whole world as a market. This conclusion opens the way for an explanation of the origin and use of money.

The further division of labour proceeds, the smaller the part of his wants which the produce of the individual man's labour can supply. What he has to do, is to exchange the surplus part of the produce of his own labour for such parts of the produce of other men's labour as he has occasion for. Thus every man becomes in some measure a merchant, and society itself grows to be what is properly a commercial society. But the produce of a particular kind of labour will not always suit the wants of the other man who, in his turn, has the required produce of his labour to dispose of. The baker may not at the moment require, or be capable of availing himself of, the labour of the barrister. Therefore every prudent person must naturally endeavour to manage his affairs in such a manner as to have at all times by him, besides the peculiar produce of his own industry, a certain quantity of some commodity which most people will accept in exchange for the produce of their own labour. Such commodities are the precious metals, and it is in this manner that money has become in all civilized countries the universal instrument of commerce, by the intervention of which goods of all kinds are bought and sold, or exchanged for one another. Smith sets himself, at this point, to ascertain the rules which determine the basis on which the exchange takes place ; in other words, the nature of *value.* This expression he finds has two different meanings. It expresses sometimes the utility of some particular object, and sometimes the power of purchasing other goods which the possession of that object conveys. The one may be called "value in use," the other "value in exchange." The things which have the greatest value in use, often have little or no value in exchange ; and, on the contrary, those which have the greatest value in exchange, have frequently little or no value in use. "Nothing is more useful than water; but it will purchase scarce anything; scarce anything can be had in exchange for it. A diamond, on the contrary, has scarce any value in use; but very great quantity of other goods may frequently be had in exchange for it." Wealth, as Hobbes had already shown, is the power of purchasing or commanding the produce of labour in the market. And the exchangeable value of everything must always be precisely equal to the extent of this power which it conveys to the owner. But though labour is the real measure of the exchangeable value of all commodities, it is not that by which their value is commonly estimated. It is not easy to find any accurate measure either of hardship or ingenuity.

In exchanging the different productions of different sorts of labour the one for the other, some allowance is made for both. That allowance is adjusted, however, not by any accurate measure, but by what Adam Smith, in a famous phrase, terms the higgling and bargaining of the market. And it comes to pass that the exchangeable value of any commodity is naturally more frequently estimated by the quantity of money, than by the quantity either of labour or any other commodity which can be had in exchange for it. But gold and silver themselves vary in price. They are therefore misleading as the measure of the value of commodities. Of these commodities they constitute the nominal price only; the ultimate and real price being always labour itself. It follows that equal quantities of labour will at distant times be purchased more nearly with equal quantities of corn, the subsistence of labour, than with equal quantities of gold and silver, or, perhaps, of any other commodity.

" The subsistence of the labourer, or the real price of labour, is very different upon different occasions: more liberal in a society advancing to opulence, than in one that is standing still; and in one that is standing still, than in one that is going backwards. Every other commodity, however, will at any particular time purchase a greater or smaller quantity of labour in proportion to the quantity of subsistence which it can purchase at that time. A rent, therefore, reserved in corn, is liable only to the variations in the price of labour which a certain quantity of corn can purchase. But a rent reserved in any other commodity is liable, not only to the variations of the quantity of labour which any particular quantity of corn can purchase, but to the variations in the quantity of corn which can be purchased by any particular quantity of that commodity."

Of course Smith does not intend in this passage to convey that a corn rent represents an unvarying value— the diminution in the cost of production of corn effected by improvement in agricultural methods would in itself cause such a value to vary very greatly. And he points out that a corn rent, though it varies much less from century to century, varies more from year to year. But he states the principle the best illustration of which in modern times is probably the fall in the value of silver relatively to gold, and the importation as a consequence into this country of Indian corn obtained in exchange for a relatively depreciated rupee, the purchasing power of which remains, so far as Indian labour is concerned, intact. This portion of the book concludes with a description of the system under which the gold and silver coinage of Great Britain had grown up, **and** of the existing mint regulations.

We now come to quite a different subject. **In** a primitive state of society "the whole produce of labour belongs to the labourer, and the quantity of labour commonly employed in acquiring or producing any commodity is the only circumstance which can regulate the quantity of labour which it ought commonly to purchase, command, or exchange for. But as soon as stock has accumulated in the hands of particular persons, some of them will naturally employ it in setting to work industrious people, whom they will supply with materials and subsistence, in order to make a profit by the sale of their work, or by what their labour adds to the value of the materials. In exchanging the complete manufacture either for money, for labour, or for other goods, over and above what may be sufficient to pay the price of the materials and the wages of the workmen, something must be given for the profits of the undertaker of the work who hazards his stock in this adventure. The value which the workmen add to the materials therefore resolves itself in this case into two parts, of which the one pays their wages, the other the profits of their employer upon the whole stock of materials and wages which he advanced." But it would be a fallacy to draw the inference here that the profits of stock are only, under another name, wages of that kind of labour which consists in superintendence. In many businesses the entire work of superintendence is done by a manager or clerk, whose wages are really wages of superintendence, bearing no necessary proportion to the capital under his control. In such cases the owner of the capital, though he may have no active duty to perform, still expects that his profits should bear a regular proportion to his capital. These profits are therefore regulated by principles quite different from those which govern the wages of labour of whatever kind. In his edition of the "Wealth of Nations," Professor Thorold Rogers remarks upon the passage where this doctrine is laid down, that where any profit greater than the ordinary rate of interest can be made out of a business, the superintendence of which is thus delegated, it will always be found that the business is one in which goodwill or connection, which is really a part of the capital embarked, is a conspicuous element. And he adds that the experience of joint-stock enterprise proves that, on the whole, the rate of profit attainable in such a business as can be done under the superintendence of paid officials, is not much, if at all, in excess of the ordinary rate of interest, and that the introduction of a system under which such officials are paid proportionately to profits, does not materially alter this rule, although it imparts security to the transactions entered on. It may be added, by way of comment on this, that what are called merchant's profits must consist, in cases where the merchant himself superintends the business, of the two elements of wages of superintendence and of interest on capital, such wages and interest varying with the difficulty and the risk of the undertaking.

But there is yet another deduction to be made, in a civilized country, from that which would otherwise be shared between the labourer and the capitalist. "As soon as the land of any country has all become private property, the landlords, like all other men, love to reap where they never sowed, and demand a rent even for its natural produce. The wood of the forest, the grass of the field, and all the natural fruits of the earth, which when the land was in common, cost the labourer only the trouble of gathering them, come even to him to have an additional price fixed upon them. He must then pay for the license to gather them, and must give up to the landlord a portion of what his labour either collects or produces. This portion, or what comes to the same thing, the price of this portion, constitutes the rent of land, and in the price of the greater part of the commodities makes a third component part." Whether or not we are content with the theory of rent as it was afterwards propounded by Ricardo, we must acknowledge that this is very loose reasoning in one point. In his letter of congratulation on the appearance of "The Wealth of Nations," Hume writes to Smith, "If you were here at my fireside I should dispute some of your principles. I cannot think that the rent of farms makes any part of the price of produce, but that the price is altogether determined by the quantity and the demand." Hume himself is not perfectly accurate in this suggestion, but he saw clearly that rent (and he might have added the profits of stock) in no way enter into cost of production or price. Rent is a consequence of, and not a component element in, price. One of the most remarkable of the steps in the reasoning of his great treatise is Smith's conclusion as to the nature of rent. But, as we shall see, if it is unsound it at least possesses this merit, that it is based on an observation of the facts, which relieves it of the abstract character that renders the deductive theory of Ricardo so difficult a formula to apply in the investigation of concrete cases.

In every society or neighbourhood there is an ordinary or average rate of wages, profit, and rent, which may be called the natural rate. This natural rate is determined by the general circumstances of the community. When a particular commodity is sold for what is neither more nor less than is sufficient to pay the rent of the land, the wages of labour, and the profits of the stock employed in raising, preparing, and bringing to market, according to their natural rates, the commodity is sold for what may be called, according to Smith, its natural price. But the actual price at which the commodity is sold may be either above, or below, or exactly equal to the natural price. This actual price he terms the market price. The market price of every particular commodity is regulated by the proportion between the quantity which is actually brought to market, and the demand of those who are willing to pay the natural price of the commodity, or the whole value of the rent, labour, and profit which must be paid in order to bring it thither. Such people may be called effectual demanders, and their demand the effectual demand; still it may be sufficient to effectuate the bringing of the commodity to market. It is very different from the actual demand. A poor man may be said in some sense to

have a demand for a coach and six; he might like to
have it, but his demand is not an effectual demand,
as the commodity can never be brought to market in
order to satisfy it. According as the quantity of the
commodity which is brought to market falls short of,
exceeds, or is equal to, the effectual demand, the market
price exceeds, falls below, or is the same as the natural
price, which is the central price to which the market
prices are always gravitating, the variations from it falling
chiefly upon those parts of the market price which
resolve themselves into wages and profits, and least upon
rent.

This brings the inquiry to the point where it becomes
necessary to investigate the variation of the natural price
with the natural rate of each of its component parts,
wages, profits, and rent, and to determine the causes of
these different variations. Had that condition of un-
civilized existence continued, in which the whole produce
of labour goes to the labourer, all things would gradually
have become cheaper. The wages of labour would have
augmented with all those improvements in its productive
power to which the division of labour has given occasion.
"But," remarks Smith, the characteristic dislike of land-
lordism which appears throughout his book leading him
to assign a somewhat doubtful period as the origin of
private property in land, "as soon as land becomes
private property, the landlord demands a share of almost
all the produce which the labourer can either raise or
collect from it. His rent makes the first deduction from
the produce of the labour which is employed on the
land." It would be hardly less incorrect to say that

private property in land preceded agriculture. The two institutions were probably in fact contemporaneous in their origin, and have operated beneficially on each other.

He proceeds to illustrate the causes of rise in wages in a passage which is so interesting that it is worth quoting :—

"It is not the actual greatness of national wealth, but its continual increase, which occasions a rise in the wages of labour. It is not, accordingly, in the richest countries, but in the most thriving, or in those which are growing rich the fastest, that the wages of labour are highest. England is certainly, in the present times, a much richer country than any part of North America. The wages of labour, however, are much higher in North America than in any part of England. In the province of New York common labourers earn three shillings and sixpence currency, equal to two shillings sterling a day; ship carpenters, ten shillings and six-pence currency, with a pint of rum, worth sixpence sterling; house carpenters and bricklayers, eight shillings currency, equal to four shillings and sixpence sterling; journeymen tailors, five shillings currency, equal to about two shillings and tenpence sterling. These prices are all above the London price; the wages are said to be as high in the other colonies as in New York. The price of provisions is everywhere in North America much lower than in England. A dearth has never been known there. In the worst seasons they have always had a sufficiency for themselves, though less for exportation.

If the money price of labour, therefore, be higher than it
is anywhere in the mother country, its real price, the real
command of the necessaries and conveniences of life
which it conveys to the labourer, must be higher in a
still greater proportion."

He proceeds to point out the conditions under which
there might arise a pressure of population upon the
means of subsistence, in a passage which contains the
foundation upon which the Malthusian theory of population was based. He reminds us that even when the
wealth of a country is very great, still, if that country be
stationary, we must not expect to find wages high in it.
The funds, he says, "destined for the payment of wages,
the revenue and stock of its inhabitants, may be of the
greatest extent, but if they have continued for several
centuries of the same, or nearly the same, extent, the
number of labourers employed every year could easily
supply, and even more than supply, the number wanted
the following year. There could seldom be any scarcity
of hands, nor could the masters be obliged to bid one
against the other in order to get them. The hands, on
the contrary, would in this case naturally multiply beyond
their employment. There would be a constant scarcity
of employment, and the labourers would be obliged to
bid one against the other in order to get it. If in such
a country the wages of labour had ever been more than
sufficient to maintain the labourer, and to enable him to
bring up a family, the competition of the labourers and
the interest of the masters would soon reduce them to
the lowest rate which is consistent with humanity. This

proposition he proceeds to illustrate at some length by a description of the state of the labour market in China. But bad as he finds the condition of China to be, he considers that of Bengal to be worse. Here the funds destined for the maintenance of labour are not only not increasing, but are, in his judgment, decreasing.

"In a fertile country, which had before been much depopulated, where subsistence, consequently, should not be very difficult, and where, notwithstanding, three or four hundred thousand people die of hunger in one year, we may be assured that the funds destined for the maintenance of the labouring poor are fast decaying. The difference between the genius of the British Constitution, which protects and governs North America, and that of the mercantile company which oppresses and domineers in the East Indies, cannot, perhaps, be better illustrated than by the different state of those countries."

And then he sums up :—

"The liberal reward of labour, therefore, as it is the necessary effect, so it is the natural symptom of increasing national wealth. The scanty maintenance of the labouring poor, on the other hand, is the natural symptom that things are at a stand, and their starving condition that they are going fast backward. In Great Britain the wages of labour seem, in the present times, to be evidently more than what is precisely necessary to enable the labourer to bring up a family. In order to satisfy ourselves upon this point, it will not be necessary to enter into any tedious or doubtful calculation of what may be

the lowest sum upon which it is possible to do this.
There are many plain symptoms that the wages
of labour are nowhere in this country regulated by
this lowest rate which is consistent with common
humanity."

After examining a number of facts bearing upon this
conclusion, Smith goes on to point out that what he calls
the liberal reward of labour is not only the effect, as we
have already seen it to be, of increasing wealth, but is the
cause of increasing population, and that to complain of
it is to lament over the necessary effect and cause of the
greatest public prosperity.

We have already remarked that in all this there is
the foundation upon which Malthus raised a theory of
society, depending upon the proposition that population
is ever tending to press upon the means of subsistence.
But although Smith recognized this doctrine also, he
characteristically regarded it as true, not in the shape of
an abstract principle, but only hypothetically, upon the
assumption of the truth of the further proposition that
society was in a stationary condition. He therefore
rejected its application to the England and Scotland of
his time. A more questionable part of his teaching is
the covert assumption of a fixed wage fund, which under-
lies the whole of this portion of his book. It is remarkable that his high sense of the necessity of reasoning
with reference to concrete facts should not have led him
to see that the proportion of the produce of labour which
goes in payment of wages is not, in point of fact, a fixed
proportion, but one which, on the contrary, is of a most

varying and inconstant character, depending on a variety of causes which alter as the constitution and character of society in general alter.

Passing from the subject of wages to that of profits, he lays down the maxim that wherever a great deal can be made by the use of money, a great deal will be given for it, and that, consequently, the ordinary rate of profit varies with the market rate of interest. He proceeds, accordingly, to form an historical estimate of the changes in the rate of profit from the regulations of the rate of interest created by the Usury laws. His investigation leads him to the conclusion that high profits tend much more to raise the price of work than do high wages. A rise in wages means only an addition to a certain part of the cost in the various stages of the process of manufacture. But if the profits of the various employers of the workmen engaged in the various stages of the manufacture of the article are raised, say 5 per cent., that part of the price of the commodity which resolves itself into profit, will, through all the stages of the manufacture, rise, not as in the case of the wages in arithmetical, but in geometrical proportion to this rise of profit. The employer of flax-dressers will, in selling his flax, require an additional 5 per cent. on the whole value of the material, and on the wages he has paid to his workmen. The employer of the spinners will require an additional 5 per cent., both upon the advanced value of the flax, and upon the wages of the spinners. And the employer of the weavers will require a like 5 per cent., both on the advanced price of the linen yarn, and on the wages of the weavers.

"In raising the price of the commodities the rise of wages operates in the same way as simple interest does in the accumulation of debt. The rise **of** profit operates like compound interest. The merchants and master-manufacturers complain much of the bad effects of high wages in raising price, and thereby lessening the sale **of** the goods both at home and abroad. They say nothing concerning the bad effects of high profits. They are silent with regard to the pernicious effects of their own gains. They complain only of those of other people." The world, at the time when Adam Smith wrote his book, was not very different from what it is to-day.

In some forms of employment the remuneration is great; in others it is small. What are the determining and counterbalancing considerations which preserve the level of demand and supply? These Smith finds to be five-fold. First, the agreeableness and disagreeableness of the employments themselves; second, the easiness and cheapness, or difficulty and expense of learning them; thirdly, the constancy or inconstancy of employment in them; fourthly, the small or great trust which must be reposed in those who exercise them; and fifthly, the probability or improbability of success in them. His remarks under these five different heads are most acute and curious, and it is to be regretted that the limits of these pages do not admit of their reproduction. One passage, however, deserves to be quoted :—

"The probability that any particular person shall ever be qualified for the employment to which he is educated, is very different in different occupations. In the greater part of mechanic trades success is almost certain, but very uncertain in the liberal professions. Put your son apprentice to a shoemaker, there is little doubt of his learning to make a pair of shoes, but send him to study the law, it is at least twenty to one if ever he makes such proficiency as will enable him to live by the business. In a perfectly fair lottery those who draw the prizes ought to gain all that is lost by those who draw the blanks. In a profession where twenty fail for one that succeeds, that one ought to gain all that should have been gained by the unsuccessful twenty. The counsellor at law, who perhaps at near forty years of age begins to make something by his profession, ought to receive the retribution, not only of his own so tedious and expensive education, but of that of more than twenty others who are never likely to make anything by it. How extravagant soever the fees of counsellors at law may sometimes appear, their real retribution is never equal to this. Compute in any particular place what is likely to be annually gained, and what is likely to be annually spent, by all the different workmen in any common trade, such as that of shoemakers or weavers, and you will find that the former sum will generally exceed the latter. But make the same computation with regard to all the counsellors and students of law in all the different inns of court, and you will find that their annual gains bear but a very small proportion to their annual expense, even though you rate the former as high and the latter as low as can well be done. The lottery of the law therefore is very far from being a perfectly fair lottery, and that, as well as many other liberal and honourable professions, are in point of pecuniary gain evidently under-recompensed.

" Those professions keep their level, however, with other occupations, and notwithstanding these discourage-ments, all the most generous and liberal spirits are eager to crowd into them. Two different causes contribute to recommend them. First, the desire **of** the reputation which attends upon superior excellence in any of them ; and, secondly, the natural confidence which every man has more or less not only in his own abilities, but in his own good fortune.

"To excel in any profession in which but few arrive at mediocrity, is the most decisive mark of what is called genius or superior talents. The public admiration, which attends upon such distinguished abilities, makes always a part of their reward ; a greater or smaller in proportion as it is higher or lower in degree. It makes a consider-able part of that reward in the profession of physic ; a still greater perhaps in that of law; in poetry and philo-sophy it makes almost the whole.

" There are some very agreeable and beautiful talents of which the possession commands a certain sort of admiration, but of which the exercise for the sake of gain is considered, whether from reason or prejudice, as a sort of public prostitution. The pecuniary recompense, therefore, of those who exercise them in this manner must be sufficient, not only to pay for the time, labour, and expense of acquiring the talents, but for the discredit which attends the employment of them as a means of subsistence. The exorbitant rewards of players, opera-singers, opera-dancers, &c., are founded upon those two principles, the rarity and beauty of the talents, and the dis-credit of employing them in this manner. It seems absurd at first sight that we should despise their persons, and yet reward their talents with the most profuse liberality. While we do the one, however, we must of necessity do the other. Should the public opinion or prejudice ever alter with regard to such occupations, their pecuniary recompense would quickly diminish. More people would apply to them, and the competition would quickly reduce the price of their labour. Such talents, though far from being common, are by no means so rare as is imagined. Many people possess them in great perfection who disdain to make this use of them, and many more are capable of acquiring them if anything could be made honourably by them.

"The over-weening conceit which the greater part of men have of their own abilities is an ancient evil remarked by the philosophers and moralists of all ages. Their absurd presumption in their own good fortune has been less taken notice of; it is, however, if possible, still more universal. There is no man living who, when in tolerable health and spirits, has not some share of it. The chance of gain is by every man more or less over-valued, and the chance of loss is by most men under-valued, and by scarce any man, who is in tolerable health and spirits, valued more than it is worth."

We now come to a part of the book where the author not only states principles, but attacks institutions. He considered—and the history of Europe during the present century has proved him to be right—that certain municipal organizations and industrial codes, which were accounted of great importance in his day, were exercising a pernicious influence. The first of these institutions with which he deals is one that has become almost entirely obsolete since he wrote, mainly owing to the success of his teaching. We associate Smith's name chiefly with his attack upon the doctrines of Protection ; we ought equally to associate it with that attack upon the exclusive trade privileges of the corporations and guilds, which, in his day, restrained competition at every turn. To become free of the trade of such a body, it was necessary to have served a long apprenticeship as one of a limited number of apprentices. By the 5th of Elizabeth, the Statute of Apprentices, it was enacted that no person should for the future exercise any trade, craft, or mystery at that time exercised in England, unless he had previously served to it an apprenticeship of seven years at least ; and what before had been the bye-law of many particular corporations, became in England the general and public law of all trades carried on in market towns. This statute has been repealed since Smith wrote, but in his time it was in full force. Its principle he exposes and denounces. He shows the futility and evil of long apprenticeships, and the bad consequences that attended the monopolies of corporations and guilds, in language which has become classical. The effect of their bye-laws and regulations he declares to be, simply to enable their members to raise their prices without the fear of being undersold, either by the free competition of their fellow-countrymen, or by foreigners. The enhanced price he finds is everywhere paid by the landlords, farmers, and labourers of the country.

The next point of attack is that policy which occasions another inequality of a different kind, by increasing the competition in some employments beyond what it would naturally be. His illustration of this is the establishment of foundations for the education and maintenance of the clergy. "Very few of them are educated at their own expense. The long, tedious, and expensive education, therefore, of those who are, will not always procure them a suitable reward, the Church being crowded with people who, in order to get employment, are willing to accept of a much smaller recompense than what such an education would otherwise have entitled them to; and in this way the competition of the poor takes away the reward of the rich." "Whenever the law has attempted to regulate the wages of workmen, it has always been rather to lower them than to raise them. But the law has upon many occasions attempted to raise the wages of curates, and, for the dignity of the Church, to oblige the rectors of parishes to give them more than the wretched maintenance which they themselves might be willing to accept of. And in both cases the law seems to have been equally ineffectual, and has never either been able to raise the wages of curates, or to sink those of labourers to the degree that was intended, because it has never been able to hinder either the one from being willing to accept of less than the legal allowance, on account of the indigence of their situation and the multitude of their competitors, or the other from receiving more, on account of the contrary competition of those who expected to derive either profit or pleasure from employing them." The following passage is of interest as showing the circumstances of the times:

"The unprosperous race of men, commonly called men of letters, are pretty much in the situation which lawyers and physicians probably would be in upon the foregoing supposition. In every part of Europe the greater part of them have been educated for the Church, but have been hindered by different reasons from entering into Holy Orders. They have generally, therefore, been educated at the public expense, and their numbers are everywhere so great as commonly to reduce the price of their labours to a very paltry recompense."

Bad as he finds the policy of the then corporation laws to be, its badness is, in his opinion, equalled, if not excelled, by the policy of the then poor laws. The obstruction to the free circulation of labour, and consequently of capital, from one employment to another, consisted here in the difficulty which a poor man found in obtaining a settlement, or even in being allowed to exercise his industry in any parish but that to which he belonged. He enters in detail into the history of the poor law, quoting largely from Burn's treatise on the subject. It is difficult to conceive anything more instructive, to the student of politics, than the study of this chapter in the light of the changes in the law which its teaching succeeded in bringing about.

The first book concludes with a lengthy statement of the theory of rent, a theory which, as propounded by Adam Smith, has been the subject of much hostile criticism at the hands of Ricardo and others. Rent, according to Smith, is to be regarded as the price paid for the use of land, and is naturally the highest which the tenant can afford to pay in the actual circumstances of the land. In adjusting the terms of the lease, the landlord endeavours to leave him no greater share of the produce than what is sufficient to keep up the stock from which he furnishes the seed, pays the labour, and purchases and maintains the cattle and other instruments of husbandry, together with the ordinary profits of farming stock in the neighbourhood. This is evidently the smallest share with which the tenant can content himself without being a loser, and the landlord seldom means to leave him any more. The rent of land, considered as the price paid for the land, is a monopoly price. It is not at all proportioned to what the landlord may have laid out upon the improvement of the land, or to what he can afford to take, but to what the farmer can afford to give. "Rent," continues Smith, "enters into the composition of the price of commodities in a different way from wages and profit. High or low wages or profit are the causes of high or low price; high or low rent is the effect of it. It is because high or low wages or profit must be paid in order to bring a particular commodity to market that its price is high or low. But it is because its price is high or low, a great deal more, or very little more, or no more than what is sufficient to pay these wages and profit, that it affords a high rent, or a low rent, or no rent at all." The first criticism to be made on this statement is that rent does not enter at all into price. Whether or not we accept Ricardo's theory of rent as a satisfactory explanation of the origin of rent—the theory that rent is the price paid, not for the mere use of the land, but for the extra fertility of the soil, which causes people to pay more for it than they would do for the worst land that will repay the cost of cultivation—at least Ricardo kept clear of the confusion which Smith's language leads him into, and which, as we have seen, Hume pointed out. Until it is understood that rent does not enter at all into cost of production, it is impossible to avoid obscurity in treating of the subject. And accordingly, acute and fertile as Smith's discussion of the theory of rent is, and based, as his conclusions are, upon observations which keep him from going far wrong, it is probable that the theoretical part of the concluding chapter of the first book is the least valuable portion of "The Wealth of Nations." The remainder of it is devoted to a history of the prices of produce, and to a digression on the variations in the proportion between the values of silver and gold.

In the first book the author dealt with the nature of profits, and their division. In the second he turns to what, throughout his work, he terms "stock," meaning by this expression capital in the widest sense in which we use the word. When the division of labour has once been thoroughly introduced, the produce of a man's own labour can supply but a small part of his occasional wants. The far greater part of them are supplied by the produce of other men's labour, which he purchases with the produce, or what is the same thing, the price of the produce, of his own. But this purchase cannot be made till such time as the produce of his own labour has not only been completed, but sold. A stock of goods of different kinds, therefore, must be stored up somewhere, sufficient to maintain him, and to supply him with the materials and tools of his own work, till such time, at least, as both these events can be brought about. As the accumulation of stock must, in the nature of things, be previous to the division of labour, so labour can be more and more subdivided in proportion only as stock is previously more and more accumulated. The quantity of materials which the same number of people can work up, increases in a great proportion as labour comes to be more and more subdivided; and as the operations of each workman are gradually reduced to a greater degree of simplicity. A variety of new machines came to be invented for facilitating and abridging these operations. As the division of labour advances, therefore, in order to give constant employment to an equal number of work-men, an equal stock of provisions and a greater stock of materials and tools than would have been necessary in a ruder state of things, must be accumulated before-hand. And the quantity of industry, not only increases in every country with the increase of the stock which employs it, but in consequence of that increase, the same quantity of industry produces a much greater quantity of work.

Certain capital is set aside as the source from which a revenue is yielded. Other part is made use of for consumption. The first kind may be used in the pur-chase and resale at a profit of goods. Such capital is always changing its form, and is called by Smith circulating capital. The second kind may be employed, for example, in the improvement of land or the establish-ment of machinery or instruments of trade; it is called

fixed capital. And just as the capital of the individual
is divided into these three kinds, so the capital of a
nation is divided into consumable, circulating, and fixed.
The first is illustrated by food, furniture, and clothes;
the second, by machinery, profitable buildings, land,
improvements, and acquired and useful abilities; the
third, by that kind of capital which, like the capital
requisite for carrying on a business, is only remunerative
in so far as it is used. These distinctions led Smith
into a discussion of the functions of money as a part of
the circulating capital of the country, and finally into an
examination of the part performed by the banking
systems of Scotland and England, a topic to which he
devotes considerable space, and which he handles from
the point of view of the practical knowledge which must
have come to him in Glasgow, as well as from that of a
theoretical economist. In this mixed kind of inquiry he
is at his very best.

He goes on to distinguish labour into productive and
unproductive, making, among other statements, the
somewhat more than questionable assertion, that the
labours of churchmen, statesmen, lawyers, physicians,
men of letters of all kinds, players, buffoons, musicians,
opera singers, and opera dancers, all stand on the same
footing, and belong to the second category. Like the
declamation of the actor, the harangue of the orator, or
the tune of the musician, he thinks that the work of all of
them perishes in the very instant of its production; for-
getting that to deny that any labour is productive which
does not give its result in a material form, is to deny the
name of wealth to anything but visible objects. In the

end, however, he returns to safer ground in his distinction between the effects of productive and unproductive expenditure.

"Whatever, therefore, we may imagine the real wealth of a country to consist in, whether in the value of the annual produce of its land and labour, as plain reason seems to dictate, or in the quantity of the precious metals which circulate within it, as vulgar prejudices suppose; in either view of the matter, every prodigal appears to be a public enemy, and every frugal man a public benefactor. The effects of misconduct are often the same as those of prodigality. Every injudicious and unsuccessful project in agriculture, mines, fisheries, trade, or manufactures, tends in the same manner to diminish the funds destined for the maintenance of productive labour. In every such project, although the capital is consumed by productive hands only, yet, as by the injudicious manner in which they are employed, they do not reproduce the full value of their consumption, there must always be some diminution in what would otherwise have been the productive funds of the society."

Smith passes on from this subject to examine and demolish the crude notion, put forward by no less eminent men than Locke and Montesquieu, that the increase of the quantity of gold and silver, in consequence of the discovery of the Spanish West Indies, was the real cause of the lowering of the rate of interest in Europe. These metals, they said, having become of less value themselves, the use of any particular portion of them necessarily became of less value too, and consequently the price which could be paid for it. Smith points out conclusively that, whatever were the causes which lowered the value of the capital, these causes must necessarily have lowered that of the interest in exactly the same proportion, and that the only effect of the increase in the amount of the precious metals was to diminish the value of the metals themselves.

Remarking that no kind of labour and expenditure of capital is more really productive than that which takes place in agriculture, he traces the principal cause of the rapid progress of our American colonies to the fact that their capital has mainly been employed in agriculture. But productive as agriculture is, its profits have, apparently, so far as Europe is concerned, no superiority over those of other employments. For he records that, even in his time, notwithstanding the proposals and promises of projectors, there was no instance on record of a great fortune acquired by agriculture.

The third book is almost purely historical, and need not be noticed at length here. In it he proceeds to state the natural course of things to be the direction of the greater part of the capital of every growing society— first, to agriculture ; secondly, to manufactures ; and last of all, to foreign commerce. But though this natural order of things must, he thinks, have taken place in some degree in every such society, it has, in all the modern states of Europe, been in many respects entirely inverted. The foreign commerce of some of their cities has introduced all their finer manufactures, or such as were fit for distant sale; and manufactures and foreign commerce together have given birth to the principal improvements of agriculture. The manners and customs which the nature of their original government introduced, and which remained after that government was greatly altered, necessarily forced them into this unnatural and retrograde order.

He goes on to give, at some length, reasons for thinking that, since the downfall of the Roman Empire, the policy of Europe has been more favourable to arts, manufactures, and commerce, the industry of the towns, than to agriculture, the industry of the country. In a part of this book—which consists too much of detail to be reproduced here—he traces the origin of primogeniture and entail to the desire to keep the land under the control of one powerful hand in barbarous and disorderly times, a desire which remained, though without a justification, as civilization advanced. The origin of the practice of granting leases to tenants he finds in the circumstance that, by degrees, it became more and more necessary to protect the tenant against the growing necessities of the landlord class, which led them to raise rents after a fashion unknown to their forefathers.

In the early part of this chapter some account was given of Smith's arguments against the mercantile and agricultural systems, and it is not, therefore, necessary to analyse that portion of the fourth book which deals with them. But no account of that book would be complete which omitted to notice the chapters which deal with the true principles of colonial policy.

The establishment of the European colonies in the

West Indies and America did not, he thinks, arise from that pressure of population on territorial limits which led to the colonial expansion of Greece and Rome. The hope of gain, especially through the discovery of gold and silver mines, gave the real initiative to the policy of conquest in the former case. But whatever the cause of the foundation of these colonies, unquestionably that foundation has been attended with great advantage to all parties. The enormous amount of land available in a new country sends labour up to a premium. With high wages, population tends to increase rapidly. Although wages are high, still they constitute almost the entire price of the land, and are therefore not excessive.

Thus it is that colonies have developed and flourish. But they have done so in spite of the policy which the mother country forced upon them at the time when Smith wrote. On no subject is he more pronounced and severe than upon the protective and restrictive regulations of the commerce of the time.

" When those establishments had been effectuated, and had become so considerable as to attract the attention of the mother country, the first regulations which she made with regard to them had always in view to secure to herself the monopoly of their commerce, to confine their market and to enlarge her own at their expense; and, consequently, rather to damp and discourage than to quicken and forward the course of their prosperity. In the different ways in which this monopoly has been exercised consists one of the most essential differences in the policy of the different European nations with regard to their colonies. The best of them all, that of England, is only somewhat less illiberal and oppressive than that of the rest. In what way, therefore, has the policy of Europe contributed either to the first establishment or to the present grandeur of the colonies of America? In one way, and one way only, it has contributed a good deal. *Magna virûm mater !* It bred and formed the men who were capable of achieving such great actions, and of laying the foundation of so great an empire; and there is no other quarter of the world of which the policy is capable of forming, or has ever actually and in fact formed such men. The colonies owe to the policy of Europe the education and great views of their active and enterprising founders; and some of the greatest and most important of them, so far as concerns their internal government, owe to it scarce anything else."

On the other hand, while he thinks that the mother countries derive, in the form not merely of new markets, but of increased support, great advantages from their colonies, he points out that an exclusive policy in colonial commerce is attended with considerable dangers. In the case of Great Britain, for example, the monopoly of the colony trade had, in his opinion, forced towards it so much greater a proportion of capital than it would naturally have attracted, that it had seriously disturbed the natural balance which would otherwise have taken place between the different branches of British industry. Her commerce had thus become directed principally into a single channel, and he likens her condition to that of an unwholesome body, in which some of the vital parts have become overgrown, and which, upon that account, has become liable to many dangerous disorders scarce incident to the body in which all the parts are properly proportioned. The only remedy for all this he sees in moderate and gradual relaxation of the laws which in his time gave to Great Britain the exclusive trade to the colonies, until that trade could be rendered altogether free. It is characteristic of Smith that he here advocates his Free Trade policy as one to be adopted with moderation and caution. But he is none the less bitterly impatient of any hesitation about such a policy in the interests of the mercantile section of the community. "To found a great empire for the sole purpose of raising up a people of customers, may at first sight appear a project fit only for a nation of shopkeepers. It is, however, a project altogether unfit for a nation of shopkeepers, but extremely fit for a nation whose government is influenced by shopkeepers. Such statesmen, and such statesmen only, are capable of fancying that they will find some advantage in employing the blood and treasure of their fellow-citizens to found and maintain such an empire."

In the fourth book, after concluding his denunciation of the mercantile system, and having examined in a somewhat more tender spirit, the agricultural system, he concludes by showing that the latter, by encouraging agriculture unduly in order to promote it through the medium of restraints on manufactures and foreign trade, defeats its own object, and indirectly discourages that very system of industry which it means to further. The true policy, therefore, is one of natural liberty. Every man, so long as he does not violate the laws of justice, should be left perfectly free to pursue his own interest in his own way, and to bring both his industry and his capital into competition with those of any other man or order of men. The sovereign should be completely discharged from a duty, in attempting to perform which he must always be exposed to innumerable delusions, and for the proper performance of which no human wisdom or knowledge could ever be sufficient—the duty of superintending the industry of private people, and of directing it towards employments most suitable to the interests of society. Such is the individualism of Adam Smith. But it is an individualism of no dogmatic type. It is rather the result of a close study of actual men and things, the result of the vicarious experience of one who had found that, as a general rule, the affairs of the world were best managed when the people whom these affairs concerned were left as much as possible to their own devices.

According to this system of natural liberty, the sovereign has only three duties to attend to; three duties of great importance indeed, but plain and intelligible to common understandings : first, the duty of protecting society from the violence and invasion of other independent societies; secondly, the duty of protecting, so far as possible, every member of society from the injustice or oppression of every other member of it, or the duty of establishing an exact administration of justice ; and, thirdly, the duty of erecting and maintaining certain public works and certain public institutions which it can never be for the interest of any individual, or small number of individuals, to erect and maintain, because the profit could never repay the expense to any individual, or small number of individuals, though it may frequently do much more than repay it to a great society.

The proper performance of these several duties of the sovereign necessarily supposes a certain expense, and this expense again necessarily requires a certain revenue to support it. The fifth and concluding book of "The Wealth of Nations" therefore seeks to explain, first, what are the necessary expenses of the sovereign or commonwealth; and which of those expenses ought to be defrayed by the general contribution of the whole society, and which of them by that of some particular part or members only; secondly, the various methods by which this contribution can be levied; and, thirdly, the circumstances under which incumbrances on the general revenue, or national debts, have been created. The portions of this book which deal with the expenses of defence, and of the administration of justice, do not require notice here. They are of a nature largely historical, and there is not much that is specially characteristic of their author in them. The parts, however, which deal with the public means of facilitating the commerce of society, are full of practical bearing on the legislation of his time. In them Smith subjects to a minute examination such questions as the policy of levying tolls at turnpikes, and the justice of a carriage tax. Of such tolls and taxes he complains that, in so far as they were regulated in proportion to the weight and not the value of the goods affected by them, they fell mainly upon coarse and bulky, and not on valuable commodities, and were therefore paid, not by the rich, but by the poor. In this connection he comes to the conclusion that it would not be desirable that the maintenance of the public highways should be in the hands, either of Government, who might be tempted to draw too high a revenue from the levy in respect of them, or of private individuals who, having a kind of monopoly, would be tempted to neglect their maintenance. He thinks that the best system is that of management by public commissioners or trustees, a conclusion which modern experience has borne out, and recent legislation has acted on. But his chief criticism in this part of his work is on the policy which had led the legislature in his time to confer on certain favoured corporations trade monopolies, in consideration of their undertaking the performance of duties which were properly discharged by the sovereign, such as the protection of those exercising particular kinds of trade. After examining, in a somewhat hostile spirit, the history of certain well-known regulated companies of his time, and criticising by the way, and as an incidental matter, the policy which dismembered Gibraltar from the Spanish monarchy, a dismemberment which "perhaps never served any other real purpose than to alienate from England her natural ally the King of Spain, and to unite the two principal branches of the House of Bourbon in a much stricter and more permanent alliance than the ties of blood could ever have united them,"—he comes to the East India Company. His verdict on this corporation, then in the zenith of its greatness, he gives in these words :—

"But it seems impossible, by any alterations, to render these courts," (the Courts of the proprietors and directors of the Company,) "in any respect fit to govern, or even to share in the government of a great empire ; because the greater part of their members must always have too little interest in the prosperity of that empire to give any serious attention to what may promote it. Frequently a man of great, sometimes even a man of small, fortune is willing to purchase a thousand pounds' share in India Stock, merely for the interest which he expects to acquire by a vote in the Court of proprietors. It gives him a share, though not in the plunder, yet in the appointment of the plunderers of India; the Court of directors, though they make the appointment, being necessarily more or less under the influence of the proprietors, who not only elect these directors, but sometimes overrule the appointments of their servants in India. Provided he can enjoy this influence for a few years, and thereby provide for a certain number of his friends, he frequently cares little about the dividend, or even about the value of the stock on which his vote is founded. About the prosperity of the great empire, in the government of which that vote gives him a share, he seldom cares at all. No other sovereigns ever were, or, from the nature of things, ever could be, so perfectly indifferent about the happiness or misery of their subjects, the improvement or waste of their dominions, the glory or disgrace of their administration, as, from irresistible moral causes, the greater part of the proprietors of such a mercantile company are, and necessarily must be."

The next branch of the subject with which he deals is that which relates to public institutions for purposes of instruction. He begins this inquiry by asking the question whether educational endowments have fulfilled their purpose. Now in every profession the exertion of the greater part of those who exercise it is always in proportion to the necessity they are under of making that exertion. But that necessity, to be really effectual, must not, as the bad example of the French Universities had convinced Smith, be an arbitrary and extraneous compulsion by an independent authority. If, as he thinks, endowments diminish the necessity of application in the teachers, the requisite motive can be supplied by making success depend upon effort, in the same way as it does, for example, in the profession of the law. Whatever forces a certain number of students to any college or university, independent of the merit or reputation of the teachers, tends more or less to diminish the necessity for that merit or reputation. The result is that the discipline of the universities in his time appeared to Smith to be contrived, not for the benefit of the students, but for the ease of the masters. The only real argument in favour of the universities is that, badly as things are taught there, but for these institutions they would not have been taught at all.

The chief defects in the university education of his time he traces to the circumstance that university education was originally intended only for the preparation of the clergy. The result of this was that, even in his time, the system was not well adapted to its end, and a vicious alternative of travel had been generally adopted.

" In England it becomes every day more and more

the custom to send young people to travel in foreign countries immediately upon their leaving school, and without sending them to any university. Our young people, it is said, generally return home much improved by their travels. A young man who goes abroad at seventeen or eighteen and returns home at one and twenty, returns three or four years older than he was when he went abroad ; and at that age it is very difficult not to improve a good deal in three or four years. In the course of his travels he generally acquires some knowledge of one or two foreign languages ; a knowledge, however, which is seldom sufficient to enable him either to speak or write them with propriety. In other respects he commonly returns home more conceited, more un-principled, more dissipated, and more incapable of any serious application, either to study or to business, than he could well have become in so short a time had he lived at home. By travelling so very young, by spending in the most frivolous dissipation the most precious years of his life, at a distance from the inspection and control of his parents and relations, every useful habit which the earlier parts of his education might have had some tendency to form in him, instead of being riveted and confirmed, is almost necessarily either weakened or effaced. Nothing but the discredit into which the universities are allowing themselves to fall could ever have brought into repute so very absurd a practice as that of travelling at this early period of life. By sending his son abroad a father delivers himself, at least for some time, from so disagreeable an object as that of a son unemployed, neglected, or going to ruin before his eyes."

Very much to the disadvantage of the former, he contrasts with the position of the modern public teacher that of the public teachers of ancient Greece and Rome. The reason why men of the enthusiasm, the industry, and the position of the latter, do not exist in modern times, he finds in the endowments of our modern schools and colleges, which have not only, in his opinion, corrupted the diligence of good teachers, but have rendered it almost impossible, by what is in effect a most injurious system of bounties, to have good private teachers. Greatly, he thinks, to their advantage, the absence of public institutions for the education of women prevents their time being wasted in useless kinds of study. "In every part of her life a woman feels some conveniency or advantage from every part of her education. It seldom happens that a man, in any part of his life, derives any conveniency or advantage from some of the most laborious and troublesome parts of his education."

All this does not mean that the State is to abstain from interfering for educational purposes. It should only abstain from interfering improperly. In the case of the poorer classes Smith is clear that it is the duty of the State to facilitate education by the establishment of parish or district schools, and by giving small premiums to the children who excel in them. On the grounds for such interference his language is unmistakable :—

"A man, without the proper use of the intellectual faculties of a man, is, if possible, more contemptible than a coward, and seems to be mutilated and deformed in a still more essential part of the character of human nature. Though the State was to derive no advantage from the instruction of the inferior ranks of people, it would still deserve its attention that they should not be altogether uninstructed. The State, however, derives no inconsiderable advantage from their instruction. The more they are instructed, the less liable they are to the delusions of enthusiasm and superstition which, among ignorant nations, frequently occasion the most dreadful disorders. An instructed and intelligent people, besides, are always more decent and orderly than an ignorant and stupid one. They feel themselves, each individually, more respectable, and more likely to obtain the respect of their lawful superiors, and they are therefore more disposed to respect those superiors. They are more disposed to examine, and more capable of seeing through, the interested complaints of faction and sedition, and they are, upon that account, less apt to be misled into any wanton or unnecessary opposition to the measures of government. In free countries, where the safety of government depends very much upon the favourable judgment which the people may form of its conduct, it must surely be of the greatest importance that they should not be disposed to judge rashly or capriciously concerning it."

Upon the second branch of the subject of public educational institutions, that of religious establishments, Smith is characteristically cautious. He quotes his friend Hume, " by far the most illustrious philosopher of the present age," for the proposition that the interested diligence of competition among the clergy, which would be furthered by the absence of State interference in religion is, in this case, unlike that of secular education, what every wise legislator will study to prevent, because in every "religion except the true, it is highly pernicious, and it has even a natural tendency to pervert the true by infusing into it a strong mixture of superstition, folly, and delusion." But he remarks on Hume's statement that it is at least clear that whatever may have been the good or bad effects of endowments, they were not bestowed with any view to these effects. They originated, he says, in the partizanship of political faction. And he expresses the opinion that, in the absence of this partizanship, the various sects would have lived peaceably side by side, and the dangers which Hume feared from competition among them would have been averted. In such a case no establishment would have been needed, and even if, he says, in the spirit of a true Scotch moderate of the eighteenth century, there had been any "unsocial or disagreeably rigorous on the morals of all the little sects into which the country would have been divided," the State could have put this right by means of two remedies. The first of these is the promotion of the study of science and philosophy, "the great antidote to the poison of enthusiasm and superstition." The second is even more curious, and recalls to the reader of "The Wealth of Nations" the times of the Stuarts. It is "the frequency and gaiety of public diversions."

"The State, by encouraging, that is, by giving entire liberty to all those who for their own interest would attempt, without scandal or indecency, to amuse and divert the people by painting, poetry, music, dancing, by all sorts of dramatic representations and exhibitions, would easily dissipate, in the greater part of them, that melancholy and gloomy humour which is almost always the nurse of popular superstition and enthusiasm. Public diversions have always been the objects of dread hatred to all the fanatical promoters of these popular frenzies. The gaiety and good-humour which those diversions inspire were altogether inconsistent with that temper of mind which was fittest to their purpose, or which they could best work upon. Dramatic representations, besides frequently exposing their artifices to public ridicule, and sometimes even to public execration, were upon that account, more than all other diversions, the objects of their peculiar abhorrence."

Having thus curiously proposed an alternative to re-ligious establishments, he goes on to inquire under what conditions establishments, if they must exist, are most tolerable. These he finds in equality of benefices and small endowments. Such a state of things promotes those exemplary morals which alone can give dignity to the man of small fortune. This he finds to be the reason why the Presbyterian clergy of Scotland have, as he thinks, acquired more influence over the minds of the common people than the clergy of any other established church.

The general conclusion which he draws from all this is, that the expense of the institutions for education and religious instruction may, as being beneficial to society, like that of the maintenance of justice, and, as he shows, of the maintenance of the dignity of the chief magistrate, be defrayed by a general contribution. Yet he qualifies this by adding, somewhat inconsistently, that in the first case the expense might perhaps, with equal propriety and advantage, be defrayed by those who receive the immediate benefit of such education and instruction, or by the voluntary contributions of those who think they have occasion for either the one or the other. But in the case of what are really local or provincial institutions— for example, local police—the expense ought to be borne by the local revenue only.

The main subject of interest in the rest of the book is that of taxation, a subject on which Smith's views have, in the main, become part of the traditions of orthodoxy. He begins by pointing out that the revenue of the sovereign, like that of the subject, must be derived either from stock, as, *e.g.*, in the case of the Post Office, or from land, as in the case of the land-tax. He divides taxes according as it is intended they should fall—on rent, or on profits, or on wages, or on all three indifferently. He then goes on to lay down four maxims with regard to taxation ; first, that every subject ought to contribute in proportion to his capacity, by which he means the revenue which that subject enjoys under the protection of the State. Secondly, that the tax ought to be certain, and not arbitrary. Thirdly, that every tax ought to be levied at the time, or in the manner, in which it is likely to be most convenient for the contributor to pay. And fourthly, that every tax ought to be so contrived as both to take out and to keep out of the pockets of the people as little

as possible over and above what it brings into the public
treasury, a maxim which strikes at every instance of
indirect taxation. Against the first of these canons, the
land-tax, in so far as the valuations in the various
counties and parishes are dissimilar, offends. And
tithes are equally objectionable, inasmuch as a certain
portion of the produce is, in different situations, equivalent to a different portion of the rent. Convert the
tithe into a rent-charge, and you are again face to face
with the vice of a land-tax. But, excepting in the particular aspect which he points out, a land-tax is theo-
retically unobjectionable, and he suggests that the defect
which characterizes it in this country under the existing
system might be completely remedied by a proper system
of official valuations of the land from time to time.
Indeed, ground-rents and the ordinary rent of land are,
in Smith's opinion, the most suitable species of revenue
for taxation, in so far as the owner enjoys them without
the necessity of care and attention, and no industry is
therefore discouraged by their imposition. But it must
be remembered that no tax can properly be levied on
this, any more than on other kinds of revenues, which
does not conform to the maxim of equality in its in-
cidence.

His views upon such subjects as taxes on the income
or corpus of personal property, and taxes upon such
subjects as, for example, shops, are exactly the current
views of to-day. The former he objects to as in the
nature of an inquisition ; the latter as being in the
nature of an indirect imposition on persons other than
those who pay it. In a similar fashion he examines a

very large number of the taxes of his time, both home
and foreign, in the light of his four maxims.   The
chapter is one not merely of a theoretical interest, but
of close bearing upon a variety of propositions which
are accepted by modern British statesmen, propositions
about which Smith, whatever his bias (and against private
owners of land it certainly is considerable), is everywhere
judicially impartial.

Several curious passages, curious because of the
interest which always attaches to proposals upon which
the experience of a century has cast light, deserve to be
quoted in their entirety.   We give them as the conclusion
of this account of the contents of " The Wealth of
Nations " :—

"During the most profound peace, various events
occur which require an extraordinary expense, and
Government finds it always more convenient to defray
this expense by misapplying the sinking fund than by
imposing a new tax.   Every new tax is immediately felt
more or less by the people.   It occasions always some
murmur, and meets with some opposition.   The more
taxes may have been multiplied, the higher they may
have been raised upon every different subject of taxation,
the more loudly the people complain of every new tax,
the more difficult it becomes, too, either to find out new
subjects of taxation, or to raise much higher the taxes
already imposed upon the old.   A momentary sus-
pension of the payment of debt is not immediately
felt by the people, and occasions neither murmur nor
complaint.   To borrow of the sinking fund is always an

obvious and easy expedient for getting out of the present difficulty. The more the public debts may have been accumulated, the more necessary it may have become a study to reduce them, the more dangerous, the more ruinous, it may be to misapply any part of the sinking fund, the less likely is the public debt to be reduced to any considerable degree, the more likely, the more certainly is the sinking fund to be misapplied towards defraying all the extraordinary expenses which occur in time of peace. When a nation is already overburdened with taxes, nothing but the necessities of a new war, nothing but the animosity of national vengeance, or the anxiety for national security, can induce the people to submit with tolerable patience to a new tax. Hence the usual misapplication of the sinking fund.

"In Great Britain, from the time that we had first recourse to the ruinous expedient of perpetual funding, the reduction of the public debt in time of peace has never borne any proportion to its accumulation in time of war. It was in the war which began in 1688, and was concluded by the treaty of Ryswick, in 1697, that the foundation of the present enormous debt of Great Britain was first laid."

"By a union with Great Britain, Ireland would gain, besides the freedom of trade, other advantages much more important, and which would much more than compensate any increase of taxes that might accompany that union. By the union with England the middling and inferior ranks of people in Scotland gained a complete deliverance from the power of an aristocracy which had always before oppressed them. By a union with Great Britain the greater part of the people of all ranks in Ireland would gain an equally complete deliverance from a much more oppressive aristocracy, an aristocracy not founded, like that of Scotland, in the natural and respectable distinctions of birth and fortune, but in the most odious of all distinctions, those of religious and political prejudices—distinctions which, more than any other, animate both the insolence of the oppressors and the hatred and indignation of the oppressed, and which commonly render the inhabitants of the same country more hostile to one another than those of different countries ever are. Without a union with Great Britain the inhabitants of Ireland are not likely for many ages to consider themselves as one people."

" If it should be found impracticable for Great Britain to draw any considerable augmentation of revenue from any of the resources above mentioned, the only resource which can remain to her is a diminution of her expense. In the mode of collecting and in that of expending the public revenue, though in both there may be still more improvement, Great Britain seems to be at least as economical as any of her neighbours. The military establishment which she maintains for her own defence in time of peace is more moderate than that of any European State which can pretend to rival her either in wealth or in power. None of those articles therefore seem to admit of any considerable reduction of expense. The expense of the peace establishment of the colonies was, before the commencement of the present disturbances, very considerable, and is an expense which may, and, if no revenue can be drawn from them, ought certainly to be saved altogether. This constant expense in time of peace, though very great, is insignificant in comparison with what the defence of the colonies has cost us in time of war. The last war, which was undertaken altogether on account of the colonies, cost Great Britain, it has already been observed, upwards of ninety millions. The Spanish war of 1739 was principally undertaken on their account; in which, and in the French war that was the consequence of it, Great Britain spent upwards of forty millions, a great part of which ought justly to be charged to the colonies. In those two wars the colonies cost Great Britain much more than double the sum which the national debt amounted to before the commencement of the first of them. Had it not been for these wars, that debt might, and probably would by this time, have been completely paid; and had it not been for the colonies the former of these wars might not, and the latter certainly would not, have been undertaken. It was because the colonies were supposed to be provinces of the British Empire that this expense was laid out upon them. But countries which contribute neither revenue nor military force towards the support of the empire cannot be considered as provinces. They may, perhaps, be considered as appendages, as a sort of splendid and showy equipage of the empire. But if the empire can no longer support the expense of keeping up this equipage, it ought certainly to lay it down, and if it cannot raise its revenue in proportion to its expense, it ought at least to accommodate its expense to its revenue.

If the colonies, notwithstanding their refusal to submit to British taxes, are still to be considered as provinces of the British Empire, their defence in some future war may cost Great Britain as great an expense as it ever has done in any former war. The rulers of Great Britain have, for more than a century past, amused the people with the imagination that they possessed a great empire on the west side of the Atlantic. This empire, however, has hitherto existed in imagination only. It has hitherto been, not an empire, but the project of an empire; not a gold mine, but the project of a gold mine; a project which has cost, which continues to cost, and which, if pursued in the same way it has been hitherto, is likely to cost, immense expense, without being likely to bring any profit; for the effects of the monopoly of the colony trade, it has been shown, are, to the great body of the people, mere loss instead of profit. It is surely now time that our rulers should either realize this golden dream in which they have been indulging themselves, perhaps, as well as the people, or that they should awake from it themselves, and endeavour to awaken the people. If the project cannot be completed, it ought to be given up. If any of the provinces of the British Empire cannot be made to contribute towards the support of the whole empire, it is surely time that Great Britain should free herself from the expense of defending those provinces in time of war, and of supporting any part of their civil or military establishments in time of peace, and endeavour to accommodate her future views and designs to the real mediocrity of her circumstances."

CHAPTER V.

OCCASION has already been found to advert, in these pages, to the difference between what is called political economy and politics. The characteristic feature of the former is abstraction from all but a particular kind of motive, for example, self-interest, and the deduction of conclusions from the hypothetical premises so found. The process of induction, in so far as it finds a place, is applied in the same way. Certain features are looked at, and certain features only; others, such as the operation of custom and habit, being left out of account. The truth appears to be that this is not a characteristic peculiar to economical science. There is no department of exact knowledge which has not been built up by much the same method. Physical science deals with only one kind of the relationships of things. Anatomy, and even physiology, treat the interdependence of the parts of the organism as if that interpendence were of a mechanical character, and leave out of account what stares the observer in the face in daily life, that these parts derive their distinguishing significance from this, that they are the parts of a whole which controls them in a non-mechanical fashion.

It is one of the qualities of Adam Smith's book, a quality which is at once a virtue and a vice, that it is in a measure free from this abstract character. A virtue, because we have the sense that he is writing of real men and a real world; a vice, because the tendency to take into account a plurality of aspects occasions a confusion and absence of system. His immediate successors displayed neither the virtue nor the vice. Malthus, although he did not so entirely, as is popularly believed of him, ignore the fact that there is a moral as distinguished from a physical irreducible minimum of comfort, which forms the real limit of the increase of population,—a minimum which, just because it is of a moral nature, can be raised by education and the influence of better social surroundings,—nevertheless persisted in regarding human life as a struggle for existence, in which each seeks only his own individual ends, and in which, accordingly, no other motive can be counted on. Ricardo developed this view into a hard and fast system of premises, from which he proceeded to draw a multitude of deductions. The result has been an intense reaction against these premises.

"The only thing that interests us," writes Karl Marx, in reference to America, in his book on 'Capital,' "is the secret discovered in the New World by the political economy of the Old World, and proclaimed on the house-tops; that the capitalist mode of production and accumulation, and therefore capitalist private property, have for their fundamental condition the annihilation of self-earned private property; in other words, the expropriation of the labourer."

It will have to be recognized that political economy is either a hypothetical science, dealing only with one phase of human existence, and based upon a single set of assumptions, or that it is in the nature of an art rather than a science, and consists of a series of maxims of practice, not one of which can be applied without regard to special circumstances, or apart from a previous consideration of the end sought to be obtained.

The consequence of the attempt to follow out in practice the principles of an abstract science has been to bring into somewhat sharp contrast two opposing schools of thought. The one lays stress on the individual and his rights as such. The other looks mainly to the fact that man is man only in so far as he stands in a close relationship to his fellow men, and to what has been called a social organism, as real, because as important in its influence on the units it embraces, as those units themselves.

Smith was an individualist in the sense that he was the opponent of State interference; but if he was an advocate of the doctrine of *laissez faire*, it was not as a deduction from any abstract principle. He saw that the State interference of his time was bad, and he wrote his book with reference to his time. The truth is, that his opposition to that system of interference was based on a perception that in his day it not only missed, but was of such a character that it necessarily missed, its mark. There are indications throughout "The Wealth of Nations," such, for example, as those in the chapter on education, that, while no Socialist, he regarded it as within the proper competence of a Government to meddle with individual liberty for the better training and discipline even of full-grown men. Again, Smith was a free-trader, not because everybody was in his opinion entitled to trade on the same terms with everybody else, but because he saw that free-trade was the best way of making a nation rich. This is a fact which has been often forgotten since Smith's time. What with him was a result of observation, a rule of practice, a means to an end, has been elevated to the position of a sacred principle. The case for free-trade has been overstated. It is logically, whether practically so or not, quite conceivable that if the end be not the production, but the distribution of wealth in a particular country, its circumstances may be such as to justify protection as a means to this end. The ordinary reasons in favour of free-trade do not touch such a case. For example, if it be desirable to preserve the sugar-refining industry in a condition of prosperity in this country, even at some cost to the general body of consumers of sugar, a departure from free-trade principles would probably be necessary in order to accomplish it, a departure of a kind different from those against which Smith's reasoning is directed. Grant that it is not expedient, in the interests of the commonwealth, that the consumer should thrive at the expense of particular producers, and that an indirect tax on the consumer is justifiable, because, although wasteful, it is more willingly paid than a direct levy for the maintenance of particular manufacturers, and the case for what is called fair-trade becomes very difficult to meet. It is on this question that the battle between free-trade and protection is likely

once more to be fought out before the newly enfran-
chised electorate of this country. A very serious battle
it is likely to be. The safe ground for the free-trader to
occupy is that it is the right of the consumer to get his
goods as cheaply as possible, consistently with the welfare
of the community; that it is to the interest of the community that he should do so; and that experience has
shown that all attempts on the part of the State to interfere with the natural distribution of wealth, prove in the
result to be failures. Such a position is practically in-
distinguishable from that occupied by Adam Smith,
though some of his more extravagant disciples have
passed beyond it.

It appears then that the opposition of Adam Smith to
Government interference with foreign commerce and
Government regulation of home industry, was really based
upon practical considerations. And this is doubtless the
safest ground to take up. Experience has shown that in
nine cases out of ten the State, when it does intervene,
intervenes foolishly. But this fact is often forgotten in
the contemplation of the tenth case, when the liberty of
every man to do what he likes is working injury to the
community. On the one hand, it is clear that there
should be as little interference as possible. On the other
hand there must be some. Whether or not it is possible
to refer to an abstract principle the question of the justification for such interference in a particular instance, it
is certainly expedient not to do so. There are two
reasons for this. In the first place, as has already been
observed, hardly any political problem can be treated as
a simple illustration of a single principle. Many con-

siderations of different kinds intervene in each case. In the second place, it is highly undesirable to turn Parliament—and particularly the House of Commons—into an arena where combats in political philosophy are to be fought out. There can be no sufficient theory of the relation of the State to the individual apart from some general point of view on such philosophy. And the history of the subject, quite apart from the training of British politicians, is not such as to encourage us to hope for agreement upon any speculative basis.

The possibility of a theoretical test being thus put aside, we are face to face with the difficulty of finding a practical substitute. The only way appears to be that of Adam Smith, who discussed each case on its own merits with a strong bias, derived from experience, against enlarging the duties of the Government in cases where persons under no disability were concerned. To the evils which Smith pointed out as arising from the devolution of new duties on the State, there may be added one which is assuming serious proportions—the tendency to substitute outside protection for the safeguard of moral qualities, and the weakening of motive which is consequent upon it. In saying that the Ballot and Corrupt Practices Acts are flagrant illustrations of legislation open to grave criticism on this score, it is by no means intended to convey that these measures may not have been justifiable and necessary on a balance of considerations of expediency. But their principle ought not to be extended to any other cases where considerations of expediency do not clearly turn the balance. Parliament is likely almost immediately to be called on to deal with

a number of instances where the simple question will be
whether the existence of such considerations has been
clearly made out.   And it is doubtful whether Parliament
will give this question the deliberate and judicial consideration it deserves.   At no period in its history has
the House of Commons been under greater and more
direct pressure from the constituencies.   The increasing
practice of holding public meetings on every variety
of subject, has largely facilitated the organization of
opinion.   The result is an immense amount of pressure
upon members—pressure of a kind which is extremely
difficult to withstand.   It may be, for example, that
considerations of expediency outweigh the presumption
in favour of leaving men and women to rely on their
own moral instincts as a protection from the temptations
of the publichouse.   It may be that these considerations
are so strong as to justify, in the general interest, the
subjection of the sober section of the public to some in-
convenience for the sake of those whose motives are not
enduring enough to save them from intemperance.   However this is, it is apparent that in certain localities, at all
events, although perhaps in fewer than is sometimes
supposed, the public have come to a decision upon the
point for themselves, and have returned members to
represent their opinion upon it.   Even if returned un-
pledged, it is not easy for any one to justify, on a local
issue of fact, as distinguished from a general issue of
principle, a decision in the teeth of the opinion of a
majority of the only parties concerned.   The main difficulty is generally to find out what this opinion really is,
and to prevent decisions being come to on imperfect and

misleading evidence. It is not only in such matters as Local Option that pressure may be brought to bear under circumstances which require closer scrutiny than they generally get. Neither of the great parties in the State is free from the blame of being prone to yield unduly to influences which ought to be resisted. Each of these parties is subject to its own peculiar temptations. The Protectionist movement in the Conservative ranks is certainly not based upon any deliberate judgment about the fallacious character of the current economical reasoning. On the other hand, modern Radicalism is tinged with an element of the least well-considered Socialism. There is not the smallest appearance of a division of parties taking place, or even tending to take place, on economical grounds. The best that can be hoped for from the immediate future is that each party may, in an increasing degree, tend to fulfil the real functions of an opposition by watching closely and criticizing the tendencies of its opponents to violate the concrete maxims of such thinkers as Adam Smith. If modern politics came to be conceived from such a point of view; if the spirit and meaning of party came to be with the many what they once were with the few, and what they are to-day with fewer still, there would be much to be looked for from popular government.

A juster view of democracies than that which at this moment appears to be current with educated men throughout Europe, may recognize that the outlook is far from hopeless.

THE END.

INDEX.

B.

Berkeley, Bishop, 59
Bismarck's commercial policy, 84
Buccleuch, Duke of, placed under
Smith's care, 29, 30, 31, 33 ;
Smith appointed through his in-
fluence to be one of the Com-
missioners of Customs, 50
Buckle, his opinion of the
" Wealth of Nations," 12
Burke, 25, 57

C.

Carlyle, Alexander, his descrip-
tion of Smith, 21, 22
Clergy, effects of endowments on,
121, 141
Colbert, 83, 84
Corporation Laws, 120

D.

D'Alembert, 32

E.

East India Company, Smith's
mean opinion of, 135, 136
Education, effect of endowments
on, 137–140

F.

Ferguson, 26
Free Trade, 84, 132, 153

G.

Garrick, 49
Gibbon, 36
Glasgow University, 17 ; Smith
elected to professorship of Logic,
19, and Moral Philosophy, 19,
24, 25 ; Smith elected Lord
Rector, 54, 55

H.

Home, 24
Hume, 11, 21, 24 ; letter on
Smith's " Theory of the Moral
Sentiments," 26–30 ; letter on

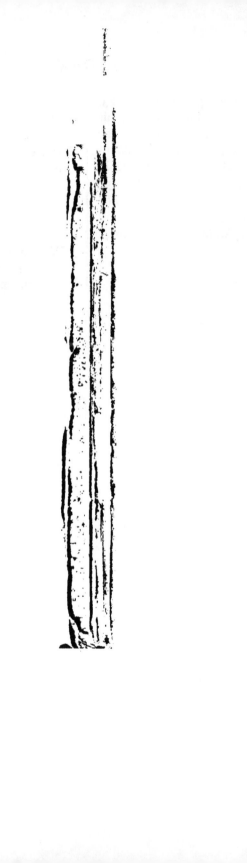

BIBLIOGRAPHY.

BY

JOHN P. ANDERSON

(British Museum).

I. WORKS.

The Works of Adam Smith, LL.D. ; with an account of his life and writings, by Dugald Stewart. 5 vols. London, 1811-12, 8vo.

II. SINGLE WORKS.

The Edinburgh Review. [To be published every six months.] Containing an account of all the books and pamphlets that have been published in Scotland from the 1st of January to the 1st of July 1755 (from July 1755 to January 1756). To each number will be given an appendix, giving an account of the books published in England and other countries that are most worthy of notice. [By Dr. W. Robertson, Dr. A. Smith, A. Wedderburn, Earl of Rosslyn, Dr. H. Blair, and others.] Nos. 1 and 2. Edinburgh, 1755 [56], 8vo.

Adam Smith contributed the article on Johnson's Dictionary, pp. 61-73, and a "Letter to the Authors of the Edinburgh Review," pp. 63-79. A second edition of this very scarce magazine, with a preface, explanatory notes, and the names of the writers of the most important articles, was published in London in 1818.

The Theory of Moral Sentiments ; or, an essay towards an analysis of the principles by which men naturally judge concerning the conduct and character, first of their neighbours, and afterwards of themselves; to which is added, a dissertation on the origin of languages, etc. London, 1759, 8vo.

——Another edition. London, 1761, 8vo.

The Theory of Moral Sentiments. Another edition. London, 1767, 8vo.

——Fourth edition. London, 1774, 8vo.

——Fifth edition. London, 1781, 8vo.

——Sixth edition, with additions and corrections. 2 vols. London, 1790, 8vo.

——Another edition. 2 vols. Basil, 1793, 8vo.

——Eighth edition. 2 vols. London, 1797, 8vo.

——Ninth edition. 2 vols. Edinburgh, 1808, 8vo.

——Twelfth edition. Glasgow, 1809, 8vo.

——Another edition. 2 vols. London, 1825, 24mo.

——Another edition. London, 1849, 8vo.

——Another edition, with a biographical and critical memoir of the author, by Dugald Stewart. (*Bohn's Standard Library.*) London, 1853, 8vo.

An Inquiry into the Nature and Causes of the Wealth of Nations. 2 vols. London, 1776, 4to.

——Second edition. 2 vols. London, 1778, 4to.

—— ——Additions and Corrections to the first and second editions of Dr. Adam Smith's Inquiry into the Nature and Causes of the Wealth of Nations. [London, 1784], 4to.

——Third edition, with additions. 3 vols. London, 1784, 8vo.

——Fifth edition. 3 vols. London, 1789, 8vo.

——Fifth edition. 2 vols. Dublin, 1793, 8vo.

——Sixth edition. 3 vols. London, 1791, 8vo.

An Inquiry into the Nature and Causes of the Wealth of Nations. Seventh edition. 3 vols. London, 1793, 8vo.

——Eighth edition. 3 vols. London, 1796, 8vo.

——Ninth edition. 3 vols. London, 1799, 8vo.

——Another edition. 4 vols in 2. Basil, 1801, 8vo.

——Tenth edition. 3 vols. London, 1802, 8vo.

——Eleventh edition, with notes, supplementary chapters, and a life of Dr. Smith, by W. Playfair. 3 vols. London, 1805, 8vo.

——Another edition, comprehending a life of the author, and a view of the doctrine of Smith compared with that of the French Economists [from the French of G. Garnier]. 3 vols. Glasgow, 1805, 8vo.

——Another edition, with a life of the author. Also, a view of the doctrine of Smith compared with that of the French Economists; with a method of facilitating the study of his works; from the French of M. Garnier. 3 vols. Edinburgh, 1806, 8vo.

——Another edition. 3 vols. London, 1812, 8vo.

—— ——A Reprint of preceding edition. London, 1870, 8vo. One of A. Murray's reprints.

—— ——Fifth edition, by A. Murray. London, 1874, 8vo. Part of a series entitled: Murray's Choice Reprints.

——A careful reprint of edition, 1812. London, [1875], 8vo. Part of a series entitled: "The World Library of Standard Books."

—— ——A reprint of the edition in 3 vols., 1812. London, [1878], 8vo.

An Inquiry into the Nature and Causes of the Wealth of Nations. Another edition, with notes and an additional volume, by D. Buchanan. 4 vols. Edinburgh, 1814, 8vo.

——Another edition, with a life of the author, an introductory discourse, notes, and supplemental dissertations. [With portrait.] By J. R. McCulloch. 4 vols. Edinburgh, 1828, 8vo.

——Another edition, with a commentary by the author of "England and America" (E. G. Wakefield. Account of the life and writings of A. S., by D. Stewart. A short view of the doctrine of Smith compared with that of the French Economists. Translated from the French of M. Garnier). 4 vols. London, 1835-39, 12mo.

> The words, "In six volumes," appear on the title-page of vol. i., but the work was completed in four. Mr. Wakefield only contributed notes to vols. i. and ii. An edition with the vols. bearing date 1840, 35, 36, 39, is a duplicate of the preceding, with a new title-page to vol. i., and without the portraits.

——Fourth edition, corrected and improved, by J. R. McCulloch. Edinburgh, 1850, 8vo.

——Another edition, by J. R. McCulloch, revised, corrected, and improved. Edinburgh. 1863, 8vo.

——Another edition. Edited by J. E. T. Rogers. 2 vols. Oxford, 1869, 8vo.

——Another edition. London [1880], 8vo.

——Another edition, with an introductory essay and notes by J. S. Nicholson. London, 1884, 8vo.

A complete analysis or abridgement of Dr. A. Smith's Inquiry into the Nature and Causes of the Wealth of Nations. By J. Joyce. Cambridge, 1797, 8vo.

——Third edition. London, 1821, 12mo.

——A Reprint of p e ed n , revised and edited r by i W. P. Emerton. 2 pts. Oxford, 1877-80, 8vo.

——An Abridgment of A. Smith's Inquiry into the Nature and Causes of the Wealth of Nations, with notes by W. P. Emerton. Oxford, 1881, 8vo.

——Analysis of A. Smith's "Wealth of Nations." Books I. and II. Arranged by F. A. B. De Wilson. Oxford, 1885, 8vo.

Essays on Philosophical Subjects. To which is prefixed an account of the life and writings of the author, by Dugald Stewart. [Edited by J. Black and J. Hutton.] London, 1795, 4to.

——Another edition. Dublin, 1795, 8vo.

——Another edition. Basil, 1799, 8vo.

Essays on i., Moral Sentiments ; ii., Astronomical Inquiries ; iii., Formation of Languages ; iv., History of Ancient Physics ; v., Ancient Logic and Metaphysics ; vi., the Imitative Arts ; vii., Music, Dancing, Poetry ; viii., the External Senses ; ix., English and Italian Verses. London, 1869, 8vo.

> One of A. Murray's Reprints.

Essays Philosophical and Literary. London [1880], 8vo.

> One of a series entitled "The World Library of Standard Works."

III. APPENDIX.

BIOGRAPHY, CRITICISM, ETC.

Agazzini, Michele.—Sconvenevolezza delle Teoriche del Valore insegnate da Smith, etc. Milano, 1834, 8vo.

Aleksyecnko, M. M.—Vzglyad na razvitie ucheniya o nalogye u ekonomistov A. Smita, Zh. B. Seya, Rikardo, Sismondi u D. S. Millya. Kharkov, 1870, 8vo.

Anderson, William.—The Scottish Nation; or, the surnames, families, literature, etc., of the people of Scotland. 3 vols. Edinburgh, 1863, 8vo.
Adam Smith, vol. iii., pp. 480-483.

Baert, J. F. B.—Adam Smith en zyn Onderzoek naar den rykdom der Volken. Leyden, 1858, 8vo.

Bagehot, Walter. — Economic Studies. Edited by Richard Holt Hutton. London, 1880, 8vo.
Adam Smith and our Modern Economy, pp. 95-134.

——Biographical Studies. Edited by Richard Holt Hutton. London, 1881, 8vo.
Adam Smith as a person, p. 247-281. Appeared originally in the Fortnightly Review, vol. xx., 1876, pp. 18-42.

Blakey, Robert.—History of Moral Science. 2 vols. London, 1833, 8vo.
Dr. Adam Smith. — Theory of Moral Sentiments, vol. ii., pp. 178-188.

Blanqui, J. A. — Histoire de l'Économie Politique en Europe, etc. 2 Tom. Paris, 1860, 12mo.
Adam Smith, Tom 2, pp. 106-120.

Boswell, James. — The Life of Samuel Johnson, LL.D., etc. With notes and appendices by A. Napier. 6 vols. London, 1884, 8vo.
In the various editions of Boswell's Johnson there are numerous references to A. S.

Brougham, Lord.—Lives of Men of Letters and Science who flourished in the time of George III. 2 vols. London, 1846, 8vo.
Adam Smith, with medallion portrait, vol. ii., pp. 86-226.

Brown, Thomas.—Lectures on the Philosophy of the Human Mind. 4 vols. Edinburgh, 1820, 8vo.
On Dr. Smith's system, vol. iv., pp. 113-158.

Buckle, Henry T.—History of Civilisation in England. New edition. 3 vols. London, 1869, 8vo.
References to A. S.

Burton, John Hill.—Life and Correspondence of David Hume. 2 vols. Edinburgh, 1846, 8vo.
Numerous references to A. S.

Cadet, Félix. — Histoire de l'économie politique. Les précurseurs: Adam Smith, Franklin. Paris, 1871, 8vo.

Carey, H. C.—Principles of Social Science. 3 vols. Philadelphia, 1877, 8vo.
Numerous references to A. S.

Carlyle, Alexander.—Autobiography of the Rev. Dr. Alexander Carlyle, etc. Edinburgh, 1860, 8vo.
Adam Smith, pp. 279-281.

Chambers, Robert.—Traditions of Edinburgh. New edition. London, 1869, 8vo.
Residence of A. Smith, p. 337.

——A biographical dictionary of eminent Scotsmen. New edition, revised by the Rev. T. Thomson. London, 1870, 8vo.
Adam Smith, vol. iii., pp. 368-376.

Chevalier, Michel.—Cours d'Économie Politique, etc. 3 Tom. Paris, 1842-50, 8vo.
Numerous references to A. S.

Chevalier. Michel. — Étude sur Adam Smith, et sur la fondation de la science économique. Paris, 1874, 8vo.

Coquelin, C. and Guillaumin, U. G. —Dictionnaire de l'Économie Politique, etc. 2 Tom. Paris, 1852-53, 8vo.
Adam Smith, with portrait, vol. ii., pp. 622-628.

Cossa, Luigi.—Guide to the Study of Political Economy. Translated from the second Italian edition. With a preface by W. Stanley Jevons. London, 1880, 8vo.
Adam Smith and his immediate successors, pp. 161-173.

Cousin, V.—Cours d' histoire de la Philosophie Morale au dix-huitième siècle, etc. 2 pts. Paris, 1839, 8vo.
Adam Smith, pt. ii., pp. 99-183.

Cunningham, George Godfrey.— The English Nation ; a History of England in the Lives of Englishmen. 5 vols. Edinburgh [1863-68], 4to.
Adam Smith, vol. iv., pp. 269-272.

Dieterici, Carolus F.—Num recte Ad. Smithius contenderit, sortem in agricultura positam et singulorum, et universorum opulentiæ esse commodissimam? Dissertatio, etc. Berolini [1858], 8vo.

Drake, Samuel Adams. — Our Great Benefactors ; short biographies, etc. Boston, 1884, 4to.
Adam Smith, pp. 49-54.

Emerton, W. P.—Questions and Answers in Political Economy, with references to Adam Smith, etc. (*Palæstra Oxoniensis.*) Oxford, 1879, 8vo.

Encyclopædia Britannica. — The Encyclopædia Britannica. Eighth edition. Edinburgh, 1860, 4to.
Article *Adam Smith*, by J. R. McCulloch, vol. xx., pp. 337-346.
——Ninth edition. Edinburgh, 1887, 4to.
Article *Adam Smith*, by J. K. Ingram, vol. xxii., pp. 169-171.

Farrer, J. A.—English Philosophers. Adam Smith (1723-1790.) London, 1881, 8vo.

Fawcett, Henry. — Manual of Political Economy. Sixth edition. London, 1883, 8vo.
Numerous references to A. S.

Franck, A. — Dictionnaire des sciences philosophiques. 6 tom. Paris, 1844-52, 8vo.
Adam Smith, tom vi., pp. 661-669.

Grant, James.—Cassell's Old and New Edinburgh. 3 vols. London, 1882, 4to.
References to A. S.

Gray, Simon.—All Classes productive of national wealth; or, the Theories of M. Quesnay, Dr. Adam Smith, and Mr. Gray concerning the various classes of men as to the production of wealth to the community, etc. London, 1840, 8vo.

Horne, George, *Bishop of Norwich.* —A Letter to Adam Smith on the life, death, and philosophy of his friend David Hume. By one of the people called Christians [G. Horne, Bishop of Norwich]. Oxford, 1777, 8vo.
——Third edition. Oxford, 1777, 8vo.
——Fourth edition. Oxford, 1784, 8vo.
——Another edition. London, 1799, 12mo.
——Another edition. London, 1804, 12mo,

Horne, George, *Bishop of Norwich.*
—A Letter to Adam Smith.
Another edition. London,
1811, 12mo.

——Another edition. London,
1819, 8vo.

——Another edition. London,
1836, 8vo.

——Letters on Infidelity. To
which is prefixed a Letter to
Dr. Adam Smith. A new
edition. Oxford, 1806, 8vo.

Hume, David.—The Life of David
Hume, written by himself.
[With a letter from Dr. A.
Smith to Mr. Strahan, upon
the death of Hume.] London,
1777, 8vo.

——An Apology for the Writings
of David Hume, to which is
added an Address to one of the
people called Christians, by way
of reply to his letter to Adam
Smith, LL.D. London, 1777,
12mo.

Inama-Sternegg, C. T. von.—
Adam Smith und die Bedeu-
tung seines "Wealth of
Nations" für die moderne
Nationalökonomie, etc. Inns-
bruck, 1876, 8vo.

Iversson, S. A.—Adam Smith,
author of an Inquiry into the
Wealth of Nations, and Thomas
Paine, author of the Decline
and Fall of the English System
of Finance. A critical essay,
etc. Germany, 1796, 8vo.

Joyce, J. — Analysis of Adam
Smith's Wealth of Nations.
London, 1818, 8vo.

Kaufmann, P.—Untersuchungen
im Gebiete der politisch en
Oekonomie, betreffend Adam
Smith's und seiner Schule
staatswirthschaftliche Grund-
sätze. Bonn, 1829-30, 8vo.

Law, Rev. James T.—The Poor
Man's Garden ; or, a few brief
rules for regulating allotments
of land to the poor, for potatoe
gardens. With remarks, and a
reference to the opinions of Dr.
Adam Smith in his "Wealth of
Nations." London, 1830, 8vo.

Leser, Emanuel.—Der Begriff des
Reichthums bei Adam Smith.
Heidelberg, 1874, 8vo.

Leslie, T. E. Cliffe.—Essays in
Political and Moral Philosophy.
London, 1879, 8vo.
The Wealth of Nations and the
Slave Power, pp. 51-61; originally
appeared in *Macmillan's Magazine*,
February 1863. The Political
Economy of Adam Smith, pp. 148-
166; originally appeared in the
Fortnightly Review, Nov. 1, 1870.

List, Friedrich. — The National
System of Political Economy.
Translated from the original
German by Sampson S. Lloyd.
London, 1885, 8vo.
References to A. S.

Lives.—Lives of Eminent Persons,
etc. (*Library of Useful Knowledge.*) London, 1833, 8vo.
Life of Adam Smith, 32 pages.

Lueder, August F. — Ueber
Nationalindustrie und Staatswirthschaft. 2 Th. Berlin,
1800-2, 8vo.
References to A. S.

M., T.—A Letter to His Grace
the Duke of Buccleuch, on
National Defence : with some
remarks on Dr. Smith's chapter
on that subject, in his book
entitled "An Enquiry into the
Nature and Causes of the
Wealth of Nations." London,
1778, 8vo.

McCosh, James. — The Scottish
Philosophy, biographical, ex-
pository, critical, etc. London,
1875, 8vo,
Adam Smith, pp. 162-173.

MacCulloch, John Ramsay. — Treatises and Essays on subjects connected with Economical Policy; with Biographical Sketches of Quesnay, A. Smith, and Ricardo. Edinburgh, 1853, 8vo.
——Second edition. Edinburgh, 1859, 8vo.
——A select collection of scarce and valuable tracts and other publications on Paper Currency, etc. Edited by J. R. McCulloch. London, 1857, 8vo.
Numerous references to A. S.

Mackintosh, Sir James.—On the progress of Ethical Philosophy chiefly during the xviith and xviiith centuries. Edited by William Whewell. Fourth edition. Edinburgh, 1872, 8vo.
Adam Smith, pp. 146-154.

Malthus, T. R.—Principles of Political Economy, etc. London, 1820, 8vo.
Numerous references to A. S.

Maurice, Frederick D.—Modern Philosophy; or, a treatise of moral and metaphysical philosophy, etc. London, 1862, 8vo.
Adam Smith, pp, 578-580.

Mill, John Stuart.—Principles of Political Economy. Sixth edition. 2 vols. London, 1865, 8vo.
References to A. S.

Moore, Thomas.—Memoirs, Journal, and Correspondence of T. Moore. Edited by Lord John Russell. 8 vols. London, 1853-56, 8vo.
References to A. S.

Neurath, Wilhelm.—Adam Smith im Lichte heutiger Staats und-Socialauffassung. Wien, 1884, 8vo.

Oncken, August.—Adam Smith in der Culturgeschichte. Wien, 1874, 8vo.

Oncken, August.— Adam Smith und Immanuel Kant. Der Einklang und das Wechselverhältniss ihrer Lehren über Sitte, Staat und Wirthschaft. Leipzig, 1877, 8vo.

Pamphleteer.—The Pamphleteer. Vols. 23 and 24. London, 1824, 8vo.
The Opinions of the late Mr. Ricardo and of Adam Smith on some of the leading Doctrines of Political Economy stated and compared, vol. xxiii., pp. 518-526, and vol. xxiv., pp. 50-58.

Partounau Du Puynode, M. G.— Études sur les principaux Economistes, Turgot, Adam Smith, Ricardo, Malthus, J. B. Say, Rossi. Paris, 1868, 8vo.

Paterson, James.—Kay's Edinburgh Portraits. 2 vols. London, 1885, 8vo.
Adam Smith, vol. 1., pp. 61-63.

Political Economy Club.—Political Economy Club (founded 1821). Revised Report of the Proceedings at the Dinner of 31st May 1876, held in celebration of the hundredth year of the publication of the "Wealth of Nations." London, 1876, 8vo.

Poor, Henry V.—Money and its Laws, embracing a history of monetary theories, etc. London, 1877, 8vo.
References to A. S.

Pownall, T.—A Letter from Governor Pownall to Adam Smith, being an examination of several points of doctrine, laid down in his "Inquiry into the Nature and Causes of the Wealth of Nations." London, 1776, 4to.

Purves, George.—All Classes productive of National Wealth; or, the Theories of M. Quesnai,

Dr. Adam Smith, etc. London, 1817, 8vo.

Rae, J.—Statement of some new principles in political economy, exposing fallacies in the "Wealth of Nations." Boston, 1834, 8vo.

Ricardo, David.—The Works of David Ricardo, etc. London, 1846, 8vo.
References to A. S.

Ricca - Salerno, G. — L'economia politica di Adamo Smith (*Archivio Giuridico*, Bologna, vol. xvii., 1876, pp. 301-320).

Roesler, Hermann. — Ueber die Grundlehren der von Adam Smith begründeten Volkswirth-schafts - theorie. Erlangen, 1868, 8vo.

——Zweite Auflage. Erlangen, 1871, 8vo.

Rogers, James E. Thorold.—Historical Gleanings, a series of sketches. Montagu, Walpole, Adam Smith, Cobbett. (First series.) London, 1869, 8vo.
Adam Smith, pp 95-137.

Roscher, Wilhelm.—System der Volkswirthschaft. Zehnte Auflage. 2 Bd. Stuttgart, 1873-75, 8vo.
Numerous References to A. S.

——Principles of Political Economy. Translated by John J. Lalor. 2 vols. New York, 1878, 8vo.

Sandelin, A. — Répertoire d' Économie Politique ancienne et moderne. 6 Tom. La Haye, 1846-48, 8vo.
Adam Smith, Tom. v., pp. 657-668.

Sartorius, Georg. — Von den Elementen des National-Reichthums und von der Staatswirthschaft, nach Adam Smith. Göttingen, 1806, 8vo.

Say, Jean Baptiste.—A Treatise on Political Economy. Translated from the fourth edition of the French, by C. R. Prinsep. 2 vols. London, 1821, 8vo.
References to A. S.

Secondat, C., Baron de Montesquieu.—Du Subside, selon Montesquieu, Necker, Smith, etc. Paris, 1832, 8vo.

Shadwell, John L.—A System of Political Economy. London, 1877, 8vo.
Numerous references to A. S.

Sidgwick, Henry.—The Principles of Political Economy. London, 1883, 8vo.
References to A. S.

——Outlines of the History of Ethics, etc. London, 1886, 8vo.
Adam Smith, pp. 205-207, and 212.

Simpson, A. L.—Pioneers; or, biographical sketches of leaders in various paths. London, 1861, 8vo.
Pioneers of Economical Science—Adam Smith, pp. 386-408.

Sinclair, Sir John.—Memoirs of the life and works of Sir John Sinclair. By his son, the Rev. John Sinclair. 2 vols. Edinburgh, 1837, 8vo.
Anecdotes of Adam Smith, vol. i., pp. 36-43.

Skarzynski, Witold von.—Adam Smith als Moralphilosoph und Schoepfer der Nationaloekonomie. Berlin, 1878, 8vo.

Smellie, William.—Literary and Characteristical Lives of John Gregory, Henry Home, Lord Kames, David Hume, and Adam Smith, etc. Edinburgh, 1800, 8vo.

Smith, Adam.—Adam Smith and recent Finance. By the author of "Our Deficient Revenue," etc. London [1881], 8vo.

Smith, Adam. — The essential Principles of the Wealth of Nations, illustrated in opposition to some false doctrines of Dr. A. Smith and others, etc. London, 1797, 8vo.

Stanhope, Philip H., Lord Mahon. —History of England. London, 1854, 8vo.
Adam Smith, vol. vii., pp. 497, 498.

Stewart, Dugald. — Biographical Memoirs of Adam Smith, LL.D., of William Robertson, D.D., and of Thomas Reid, D.D., read before the Royal Society of Edinburgh. Now first collected into one volume, with some additional notes. Edinburgh, 1811, 4to.
Account of the life and writings of Adam Smith, with a portrait from a model by Tassie, pp. 3-152. Appeared originally in the Transactions of the Royal Society of Edinburgh, vol iii., part 1, 1793, pp. 55-537.

Stöpel, Franz.—Adam Smith im Lichte der Gegenwart. Volkswirthschaftliche Studie. Berlin, 1879, 8vo.
Appeared originally in the *Merkur* for 1878.

Walker, Francis A. — Political Economy. London, 1883, 8vc.
References to A. S.

West, Sir Edward.—Price of Corn and Wages of Labour, with observations upon Dr. Smith's, Mr. Ricardo's, and Mr. Malthus's doctrines upon those subjects, etc. London, 1826, 8vo.

Wilson, Daniel. — Memorials of Edinburgh in the Olden Time. Edinburgh, 1872, 4to.
References to A. Smith.

Young, Sir William.—Corn Trade. An Examination of certain commercial principles, in their application to agriculture and the Corn Trade, as laid down in the Fourth Book of Mr. Adam Smith's Treatise on the Wealth of Nations. New edition. London, 1800, 8vo.
——Another edition. London, 1800, 8vo.
The name of Sir William Young appears on the title-page of this edition.

MAGAZINE ARTICLES.

Adam Smith.—North American Review, vol. 64, 1847, pp. 67-72.—Revue des Deux Mondes, by L. de Lavergne, Tom. 24, séconde période, 1859, pp. 893-929.—Banker's Magazine (New York), vol. 31, 1870, pp. 20-26. —Dublin University Magazine, by Eric S. Robertson, vol. 2, N.S., 1878, pp. 452-468.

——*and Highland Laird, Conversation with.* Blackwood's Edinburgh Magazine, vol. 3, 1818, pp. 419, 420.

——*and Ricardo.* Blackwood's Edinburgh Magazine, vol. 52, 1842, pp. 338-353, 457-469, 718-739.

——*and the United States.* Boston Monthly Magazine, vol. 1, 1825, pp. 517-521.

——*as a person.* Fortnightly Review, by Walter Bagehot, vol. 20, N.S., 1876, pp. 18-42; afterwards reprinted in *Economic Studies*, by W. Bagehot: same article, Littell's Living Age, vol. 130, pp. 387-402; and in the Eclectic Magazine, vol. 24, N.S., pp. 604-620.

——*Essays on Philosophical Subjects.* Monthly Review, Jan. 1797, pp. 57-68; May 1797, pp. 18-34 and June 1797, pp. 152-166.—British Critic, vol. 7,

Adam Smith—

1796, pp. 665 - 672.—London Review, Jan. 1796, pp. 13-17.

——*German Critics of.* Penn Monthly, vol. 3, 1872, pp. 586-596.

——*Political Economy of.* Fortnightly Review, by T. E. Cliffe Leslie, vol. 8, N.S., 1870, pp. 549-563.

——*Wealth of Nations.* Monthly Review, vol. 54, 1776, pp. 299-308, 455-465, and vol. 55, pp. 16-26, 81-92; vol. 72, 1785, pp. 272-279; vol. 39, N.S., 1802, pp. 509-514; vol. 50, N.S., June, 1806, pp. 121-130. — Edinburgh Review, vol. 7, 1806, pp. 470, 471, and vol. 70, 1840, pp. 426-445.—Penny Magazine, vol. 1, 1832, pp. 118-120.—Westminster Review, vol. 17, 1832, pp. 267-311.—Museum, vol. 22, pp. 548, etc., and 661, etc.—Monthly Review, vol. 1, N.S., 1844, pp. 368-381. — Banker's Magazine (New York),

Adam Smith—

from *Bohn's Standard Cyclopædia*, vol. 4, 1849, pp. 130-138.

—— ——*Centenary of Wealth of Nations.* Economist, June 3, 1876.—Times, June 1 and 6, 1876.—Daily News, June 1, 1876.—Pall Mall Gazette, May 30, 1876.—Capital and Labour, June 7, 1876.—Banker's Magazine (New York), vol. 31, 1876, pp. 185-190, and vol. 36, 1876, pp. 610-634.

—— ——*Wealth of Nations and the Slave Trade.* Macmillan's Magazine, by T. E. Cliffe Leslie, vol. 7, 1863, pp. 269-276; afterwards reprinted in *Essays in Political and Moral Philosophy*, by T. E. C. Leslie; same article, Eclectic Magazine, vol. 58, pp. 444-450.

——*Theory of Moral Sentiments.* Monthly Review, vol. 21, 1759, pp. 1-18, and Feb. 1791, pp. 138-142.—North American Review, vol. 8, 1819, pp. 371-396.

IV.—CHRONOLOGICAL LIST OF WORKS.

The Monthly Chronicle

OF NORTH-COUNTRY LORE AND LEGEND.

Crown Quarto, Forty-Eight Pages, Price Sixpence.

THE MONTHLY CHRONICLE has been established to preserve the great wealth of legend and story that abounds in the North of England. Every number contains a variety of articles of great popular interest. Most of the articles are illustrated with engravings of the persons or scenes described.

OPINIONS OF THE PRESS.

"A word of welcome is due to the *Monthly Chronicle of North-Country Lore and Legend*, which promises to be useful, and is certainly very cheap."—*Athenæum.*

"The *Monthly Chronicle* is an admirable sixpenny budget of North-Country lore and legend. It merits, and will doutless obtain, an extensive circulation."—*Wakefield Free Press.*

"It is illustrated and clearly printed, and promises to be a choice repository for the lore of Northumbria."—*Leeds Mercury.*

"It is splendidly got up, marvellously cheap, and interesting in every page."—*British Weekly.*

"The magazine, which is excellently arranged, and beautifully printed and illustrated, contains a great mass of matter relating to men and things of the past in Northumbria. Published at sixpence a month, it is the best local periodical we have ever seen."—*Derby and Derbyshire Gazette.*

"For the modest sum of sixpence Mr. Scott gives us no less than forty-eight closely printed quarto pages of good sound prose."—*Kelso Mail.*

"The *Monthly Chronicle* is a wonderful sixpennyworth, and we wish it the success it deserves."—*West Cumberland Times.*

"It is an amusing collection of antiquarian scraps, reminiscences, rhymes, and sketches."—*Manchester Guardian.*

"Full of interesting reading, to Tynesiders especially."—*Shields Daily News.*

Published for the Proprietors by Walter Scott, Newcastle and London.

100TH THOUSAND.

CROWN 8vo, 440 *PAGES, PRICE ONE SHILLING.*

THE WORLD
OF CANT.

"*Daily Telegraph.*"—"Decidedly a book with a purpose."

"*Scotsman.*"—"A vigorous, clever, and almost ferocious exposure, in the form of a story, of the numerous shams and injustices."

"*Newcastle Weekly Chronicle.*"—"Trenchant in sarcasm, warm in commendation of high purpose. . . . A somewhat *remarkable book.*"

"*London Figaro.*"—"It cannot be said that the author is partial ; clergymen and Nonconformist divines, Liberals and Conservatives, lawyers and tradesmen, all come under his lash. . . . The sketches are worth reading. Some of the characters are portrayed with considerable skill."

"May the Lord deliver us from all Cant : may the Lord, whatever else He do or forbear, teach us to look facts honestly in the face, and to beware (with a kind of shudder) of smearing them over with our despicable and damnable palaver into irrecognisability, and so falsifying the Lord's own Gospels to His unhappy blockheads of Children, all staggering down to Gehenna and the everlasting Swine's-trough, for want of Gospels.

"O Heaven ! it is the most accursed sin of man : and done everywhere at present, on the streets and high places at noonday ! Verily, seriously I say and pray as my chief orison, May the Lord deliver us from it."—*Letter from Carlyle to Emerson.*

London : WALTER SCOTT, 24 Warwick Lane, Paternoster Row.

Windsor Series of Poetical Anthologies.

Printed on Antique Paper. Crown 8vo. Bound in Blue Cloth, each with suitable Emblematic Design on Cover, Price 3s. 6d. Also in various Calf and Morocco Bindings.

Women's Voices. An Anthology of the most Characteristic Poems by English, Scotch, and Irish Women. Edited by Mrs. William Sharp.

Sonnets of this Century. With an Exhaustive and Critical Essay on the Sonnet. Edited by William Sharp.

The Children of the Poets. An Anthology from English and American Writers of Three Centuries. Edited by Professor Eric S. Robertson.

Sacred Song. A Volume of Religious Verse. Selected and arranged, with Notes, by Samuel Waddington.

A Century of Australian Song. Selected and Edited by Douglas B. W. Sladen, B.A., Oxon.

Jacobite Songs and Ballads. Selected and Edited, with Notes, by G. S. Macquoid.

Irish Minstrelsy. Edited, with Notes and Introduction, by H. Halliday Sparling.

The Sonnets of Europe. A Volume of Translations. Selected and arranged, with Notes, by Samuel Waddington.

Early English and Scottish Poetry. Selected and Edited, with Introduction and Notes, by H. Macaulay Fitzgibbon.

Ballads of the North Countrie. Edited, with Introduction, by Graham R. Tomson.

Songs and Poems of the Sea. An Anthology of Poems Descriptive of the Sea. Edited by Mrs. William Sharp.

Songs and Poems of Fairyland. An Anthology of English Fairy Poetry, selected and arranged, with an Introduction, by Arthur Edward Waite.

London : WALTER SCOTT, 24 Warwick Lane, Paternoster Row

In Two Volumes, Royal 8vo, Cloth, Gilt top, 12/6 per vol.;
Half Red Morocco, 15/- per vol.; Full Morocco,
Antique, 21/- per vol.

Chronological History

OF

NEWCASTLE-ON-TYNE
AND GATESHEAD.

14th to 16th CENTURIES.

EDITED BY RICHARD WELFORD,

AUTHOR OF "THE MONUMENTS OF ST. NICHOLAS' CHURCH,
NEWCASTLE," ETC., ETC.

Crown 8vo, Cloth Gilt, Price 7s. 6d.

NEWCASTLE TOWN.

AN ACCOUNT OF

ITS RISE AND PROGRESS:
ITS STRUGGLES AND TRIUMPHS:
AND ITS ENDING.

By R. J. CHARLETON.

WITH ILLUSTRATIONS BY R. JOBLING.

London : WALTER SCOTT, 24 Warwick Lane, Paternoster Row.

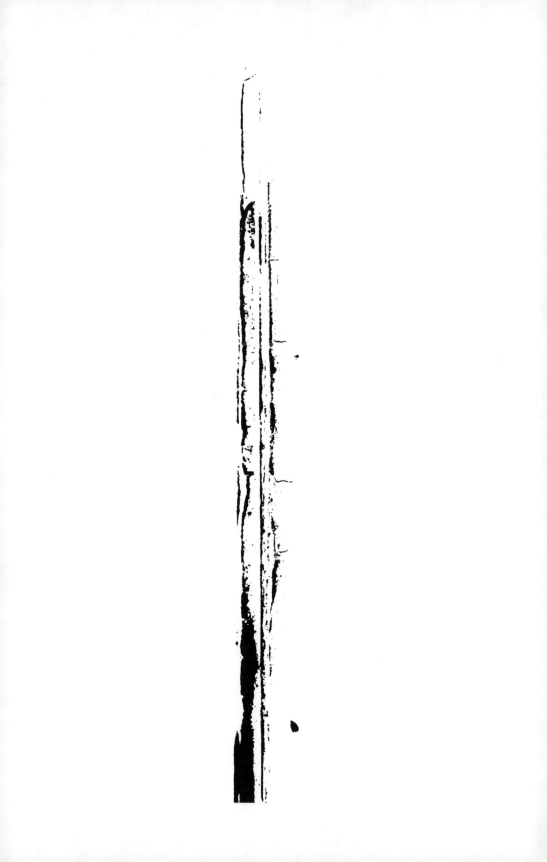